COURAGE BEYOND PASSION

Breaking Boundaries

COURAGE BEYOND PASSION: Breaking Boundaries

Copyright © 2023 By Emily Augur

All rights reserved. No part of this book may be reproduced or used in any manner except for the use of brief quotations in a book review. These are my memories from my perspective and I have tried to represent events as faithfully as possible. The information in the book was correct at the time of publication.

To request permissions, contact the publisher at kdp.amazon.com

Paperback: ISBN 9798842921010

First Paperback Edition: February 2023

Edited by: Alison Buchanan, Linda Hall Augur and Kathleen Sutherland
Cover Art by: Robert C. Augur, Jr
Interior Design by: Robert C. Augur, Jr
Text by: Emily Augur

Printed by: Kindle Direct Publishing

Published by: Kindle Direct Publishing, Columbia, SC, USA

Publisher's Website: kdp.amazon.com

Author's email: emyaugur@aol.com

Prologue

I believe that there is power in a story - in those moments woven together that define a life. A story, your story or that of another, holds within its pages the capacity to touch and impact others in dynamic life-changing ways.

I have a number of grandchildren - each one loved by me with all my heart. Each one is uniquely full of promise and potential for fine contributions to our world. Each is deserving of his or her own story. But for now, this particular story is about Johnny, my youngest grandchild, who has just crossed the threshold of the twenty-first year of his life. The purpose of writing this book is two-fold: one is that Johnny will have a record of his early years, those formative years that he might find impossible to recall. Those years were ones in which he and I spent a lot of time together - years that are written through my lenses, participations and perspectives. The second reason has been to highlight my grandson's life in order to inspire and encourage those young people, and their families, who live with the disease of Cystic Fibrosis or any other disease that is declared to be one of curbing life expectancy. I've named those the transformational years.

John Michael Kupono Buchanan, my grandson, was diagnosed with Cystic Fibrosis when he was eight months old. He has never known life without the vast array of daily medications, capsules, chest therapies, breathing treatments and periodic hospitalizations which are required in order to be engaged in the battle to survive and thrive with this unwelcome condition of CF. These treatments frequently take several hours of each day. But In spite of the constraints of CF, Johnny has never let it define who he is. From a young age, he has chosen to focus on what he can do, rather than on any negative aspects of life with CF. His boundless energy, his robust spirit, his drive to compete and succeed have demonstrated an unstoppable spirit to soar above and beyond normal patterns of living. He is filled with a joyful zest for being an all-in kind of guy, pushing beyond one hundred percent of his best. Along with a bright mind which ushers in a logical resourcefulness, Johnny is filled with humor and a remarkably contagious spirit of fun. These are the things that define him and endear him to young and old alike. How did all of these character traits come together in one young boy? How has he become so resilient? What were the factors that have contributed to his overcoming spirit and remarkable maturity?

Throughout his life, Johnny has been determined to not be in bondage to CF, but instead to accept it as a part of his life, though not a major part. He has dealt with it as his parents have modeled - as necessary to fit into his daily world and then move on and live his life as fully as his heart desires. There are lyrics to a song that are motivational to living a full life: "if you've got a dream, chase it." The Walt Disney Corporation has written, "If you can dream it, you can do it." Johnny's life has vibrantly demonstrated the belief of not shying away from risks or danger. The banner of his mind seems to have been, "dream big and go for your dreams; go all-in to achieve them."

The thrust of the book that you are holding in your hands goes beyond reaching into the heart of the one who has CF; it speaks boldly to parents and family members as well as to those young people who were born with diseases of other kinds that are considered to be somewhat debilitating. The positive attitude that parents project into the mental health and well-being of their child is monumental to their success. Well-educated understanding and optimism from parents are transmitted to their child at a young age and can free him or her to not only live a life in an attitude of optimism, but inspire them to become role models as they grow in being fully engaged in life. As a parent, walking with your child in strong participation, demonstrating a positive belief in their future, communicating your constant love for them - these building blocks will result in one of love's finest gifts, that of a living hope of a bright future. I'm rooting for you all of the way!

"One generation shall praise your works to another, and declare your mighty acts".

Psalm 145:4

Run With Me

The vineyard was large. Row after row of tall grapevines wound around rough, brown wooden stakes. The stakes were barely visible because of the leafy thick greenness of the hundreds of vines that dressed the vineyard. The rows were straight and long, covering a huge area of land. In between the rows of grapevines were paths of packed sandy-colored dirt, stretching as far as the eye could see. Johnny was fascinated by the sight. He saw the long dirt paths as a great place to run.

Johnny wore flip flops on his feet that day. I had on open-toed sandals. The long dirt paths were filled with ruts and crevices. Suddenly Johnny yelled out in his wonderfully voluminous voice, "Come on, Mimi, let's have a race. Run with me down the dirt rows." I was 77 years old – he was 10. He had nimble feet and ran like the wind. I had feet of clay, corns and calluses and couldn't run at all.

I was once again being challenged to be a playmate and what grandmother could resist that calling. We compromised! I would walk with all of the speed that I could muster and he would run as fast as he could. We would see if he made it back to the middle of the row, after having run the full length of it, before my hurried gait would enable me to even reach the middle of the row.

That day – and that race planted the seeds that took root to bring forth my book about Johnny. Our time together on that day was about a race. Johnny's life has always been about a race - a race to win breath and life and victory.

"Perfection is not attainable but if we chase it, we can catch excellence".

Vince Lombardi

Dedication

This book is dedicated to my grandson, John Michael Kupono Buchanan. It is a story, lived by him, that he has allowed me the immeasurable honor of penning. May his trust in me to write his story be equal to the challenge of capturing the invincible essence of his life, the outpourings of his phenomenal brain that never cease to astound me, as well as his remarkable talents, his courage, his unbridled joy, his zest for life, his strong Christian faith and his innate and loving kindness. I love you with all of my heart, Johnny. You are my Warrior Hero.

This book is also dedicated, In Memoriam, to my beloved husband, Robert Charles Augur. As Johnny's grandfather, he read my early manuscripts and was enthusiastic about the work. His love for, respect and admiration of Johnny, were profound and translated into his being an all-in Grandfather. It was Bob's belief that Johnny's story would be an inspirational testimony of a young man's life being extraordinarily well lived, an inspiration of motivational help to others. Johnny's mind and heart are tuned to raising the bar for victorious living. My heart speaks now to Bob, my heavenly husband, with these words - "We did it, honey - we wrote our story of Johnny. Our dream has come true! I love you always."

There is a third dedication of my heart that must be made and that is to my courageous sister, Jean

Moran. She has loved Johnny as though he were her own grandson. She is his champion in every aspect of the word and its meaning. She has lavished love, pride, humor and admiration upon Johnny all the days of his life. Johnny is her Hero, as he is mine. She, too, is a brave Warrior, one who is engaged in a life's battle. I love her dearly!

"When you were very, very small you clutched my little finger in your fist and captured me forever. You grew and learned to walk and took me off on explorations. The shabby autumn garden revealed itself as a wonderland – a last, last rose, a pigeon's feather, a fat and prosperous worm, a drift of golden leaves, a scurrying mouse. Your hands tugged me from my chair, pulled me to the door, marched me away. To the park, to the shops, to the library. The museum. The railroad. The woods. The beach. The river. Showing me a world I had half-forgotten. A world full of wonders.

And when you are grown and stride away and leave us all behind our hearts will go with you. To places we have never seen. To a time we will never know."

By Pam Brown. From "Grandmothers",
A Helen Exley Giftbook
Published 1997 by Helen Exley Publications London

Contents

Prologue
Run With Me
Dedications

Part I - The Early Years
1. The Birth of A Boy
2. Strong In Spirit
3. Spunk and Character
4. In The Moment
5. Johnny Joy
6. A Boy and A Ball
7. Bears, Penguins and Gummy Worms
8. Double Digits
9. The Redemption Tree
10. The Sound Of The Scooter
11. Make A Wish
12. Team Awesome
13. Fantasy Fun
14. The Power Of Tradition
15. A New Direction
16. Benchmark Moments

Part II - The Transformational Years
17. Unstoppable Quest
18. A Force Of Nature
19. Changes
20. A Global Invasion
21. Sorrow Strikes
22. Off To The Future
23. Catch The Vision
24. The Journey Forward

Epilogue
Acknowledgements
An Invitation
Notations

Part 1 - The Early Years

Chapter 1
THE BIRTH OF A BOY

*"The Spirit of God has made me,
and the breath of the Almighty gives me life."*
Job 33:4

It was May of 2002. My husband Bob and I were in a movie theater when the phone call came from our daughter, Alison. I stepped outside to take the call. The news was shattering – heart wrenching. The test results indicated that her son, Johnny, 8 months old then, had Cystic Fibrosis. The diagnosis had been clearly confirmed and our family began to learn what this meant. We knew it was a disease of the lungs; that it was life-threatening and incurable. But what would this mean on a daily basis in the life of Johnny and his family? Were there breakthroughs in effective treatments on the horizon, we wondered. Our minds were filled with questions that yearned for answers.

Johnny's early weeks and months following his birth on September 7, 2001, just days before the explosive devastation of September 11th, had been characterized by puzzlement on the part of his parents and pediatrician. Bouts of reflux, crying, discontentment were common – and "failure to thrive" became a familiar phrase as he didn't gain weight and weekly doctor's visits were necessary. Something was definitely wrong and it became ever more apparent as Alison took Johnny to various specialists for evaluation, tests and diagnosis. Ultimately it was a gastroenterologist who had seen Johnny one day and then awakened in the middle of that night with the thought of the possibility of Cystic Fibrosis. Early the next morning she called Alison to suggest that tests for CF be done. Tests were conducted and less than a week later, positive results on all tests confirmed a diagnosis of Cystic Fibrosis. Cystic Fibrosis (or CF) is a potentially life-threatening and unkind genetic disease that primarily affects the lungs and digestive systems. Every year in America about 1 out of every 3500 babies are born with CF. There is no cure yet, but we learned that there are daily treatments that can help to provide good quality of life for babies, children, young adults and a growing number of older adults. These treatments are time-consuming, taking as long as several hours each day. But their importance is monumental in combating potential damaging effects of the disease.

Alison and Mike vowed to do everything they could do as parents, dedicating themselves to diligently following the daily treatment procedures, to prayer, and to trusting God for the results. The amount of medications, enzymes, vitamins, minerals, bronchodilators, inhalers, etc filled kitchen cabinet shelves. Johnny, at a young age, had learned the name of each medicine and supplement as well as the prescribed dosage; his involvement astonished us. Everyone in the family was educated in the necessary regime. Johnny's brother and sister, Christopher and Emily, though young themselves, were helpful in stepping up to the plate to play games with Johnny to keep him from being bored during his chest therapy treatment times. In spite of diligence in daily treatments, infections would crop up from time to time and antibiotics would be needed. Frequent trips to a doctor were part of life, though as he grew older, the times between visits were minimized.

None of us know our future, of course, nor the length of our days on earth, but Johnny had something larger to deal with

Chapter 1

than most of us. He was daily engaged in a fight for his life. His battle had begun in 2001. 2001 was an unforgettable year in the life of our nation, for we suffered a series of blows so tragic and devastating that they changed the face of the lives of thousands of American families forever. Some are still attempting to recover. Some never will. Our family suffered that year, too. We had lost our son in March of the year, not to suicide bombers, but to the war of a life with epilepsy. Six months later, God chose to gift our family with a new baby boy – a grandson – a beautiful little boy who would begin to gently touch the cavernous void of deep, personal loss and reignite our world – reignite it with John Michael, a grandson named after our son, a son who now lived in Heaven. This new and youngest of our eight grandchildren would bring incredible joy to our lives; he would also be the reason for ongoing prayers that would keep us on our knees.

At that time, Mike and Alison were missionaries with Athletes in Action, Campus Crusade for Christ's ministry to college athletes. As a couple, they had pioneered the AIA ministry on the University of Hawaii campus, residing in Honolulu for about 10 years prior to Johnny's birth. In the ensuing months after the CF diagnosis, it was becoming increasingly apparent to them that they might want to consider relocating to a part of the United States that would offer top medical care in not only managing Cystic Fibrosis, but also one on the cutting edge of new options for treatment. The Hawaiian Islands had few children with Cystic Fibrosis and therefore, a minimal number of doctors specifically trained in the diagnosis, care and complications of the disease. There was one gifted pulmonologist that had come into Johnny's world as his primary CF care doctor. This wonderful God-given man was a Harvard graduate who had gleaned a great deal of medical experience in Boston at the Children's CF Hospital. He was reputed to be one of the leading U.S. doctors in the field, having written many papers on the disease. However there were no CF Care Centers in Honolulu, no specialized teams of trained nurses or physicians. Alison and Mike wanted the best for Johnny. They explored their options and learned that Los Angeles had an outstanding reputation for providing cutting edge care in conjunction with a state-of-the-art hospital and care center for children who have Cystic Fibrosis. Los Angeles also presented the possibility of a ministry transfer job for Mike and in addition, would provide the opportunity for the Buchanans to live near their families which would mean a strong support group of grandparents, aunts, uncles, and cousins. Such support can be invaluable in the lives of families who live daily under the cloud of a life-threatening disease. Encouragement and undergirding can make an enormous difference for parents, especially when those fragile, tough times come.

So, after much investigation and prayer, the Buchanans made the decision to return to Southern California (both had been born and raised there). This was not an easy decision for though they wanted to do whatever was best for Johnny, the whole family loved living in Hawaii. The three children had not only been born there but each bore a Hawaiian middle name. They were rooted to what is commonly called, "the tropical paradise of islands". Life on Oahu depicted small community living. Friendliness prevailed. People demonstrated a laid-back lifestyle; they had time for each other. It wasn't necessary to spend hours each day in a car, traveling to get to places. The beautiful sapphire and turquoise colors of the Pacific waters were visible around many a bend of the road and the lovely fragrance of the plumeria blossoms, as well as the soft rustling of the palm branches, enhanced the senses to embrace the pure delight of living an island life. It would be difficult to say goodbye to their ministry on the University of Hawaii campus – to

Chapter 1

the students, to their strongly cemented friendships there, to their church family, to casual living where the soft tradewinds prevailed and the cloud-adorned mountains, like a magnet, drew your eyes to behold their striking beauty. But their passion for and commitment to Johnny's well being, to giving their third-born every possible advantage to live a full life, outweighed all of the delights of island living and was, without question, their top priority. Their love for their precious son was limitless. The move would take place!

Chapter 2
STRONG IN SPIRIT

*"Your hands have made me and fashioned me, an intricate unity.
You have granted me life and favor,
and your care has preserved my spirit".*
Job 10: 8, 12

Johnny was two years old when he and his family moved to California from Honolulu. New Year's Eve of 2003 ushered in not only the new year, but also the first night that the Buchanans spent in their new home - a home where fresh adventures beckoned. It was a spacious, two-story home with a grassy backyard, a swing set, a treehouse slide – and a children's picnic table shaded by a lemon tree just bursting with juicy, ripe lemons. The promise of a puppy filled the hearts of the kids with happy anticipation – a puppy that would come to them in the springtime. The cul-de-sac neighborhood had small children and friendly families. Grandparents, aunts, uncles and cousins were not far away. New schools awaited, a new church, sports involvement and all of the offerings of the Los Angeles area. The family was excited!

One of the four bedrooms in the new house was ideal for Johnny. It was a captivating room with a high-pitched ceiling boasting a large, oak fan to bring coolness during the hot nights of summer. A ceiling border print of Noah's Ark depicting pairs of animals on board, welcomed you. A cushiony soft, green carpet graced the floor. There was a large window near Johnny's bed, making it easy to spot the moon or stars in the night sky. In the daytime, the light streamed through the window to such an extent that no artificial light was needed. The room was a playful

Chapter 2

wonderland for a young boy of Johnny's age - a room for toys, books and a game table, for imaginative puppet shows in a real marionette theater, for dinosaur battles, matchbox car racing, for bedtime stories and goodnight prayers. It was enjoyable to be in the room to let your imagination soar into the realm of "let's pretend" for a while. The only snag in the location of Johnny's room was its proximity to his sister, Emily's room. When she wasn't around, he found it almost impossible not to wander in and dig into her dinosaur collections and other prized possessions and leave things in disruption. Like with all young children, drama, tears and arguments ensued. Big brother Chris's room seemed truly off limits, in Johnny's eyes. There was that terrorizing six year difference in ages.

The childrens' wing upstairs was cozy. Bookcases were everywhere, filled with stacks of well-read books and games. There were shelves on the walls in each child's room for trophies, pictures, trinkets and treasures. Easels, chalkboards, paints and craft supplies were readily accessible - all were worn with use. This was a hands-on household, the kind of home that most children would dream of having – a home where love and creativity blended into opportunities for the kids to try new things by giving them not only the accessible items but the tools of encouragement and support as well.

In the early months after the move to California, Alison and Mike were involved in a team ministry with Athletes in Action colleagues on Mondays that necessitated their being away from home all day. These days came to be known as "Johnny Mondays". Christopher and Emily were in school so Johnny and I were Monday playmates until time to pick up the others from school. On dark or cold days we spent many hours playing in his room usually down on the floor on the soft carpet. We would set up train tracks in the center of the room and play "train" for hours. Trains would take us to destinations near and far - to "Snowball Hill", to "The Waterslide Park" and to any imaginative land. On other days it was fun to build tall towers and houses of wooden blocks, to stack them as high as we could before the buildings would begin to sway and come crashing down. Johnny liked to play anything that was active, anything where pieces fitted together, anything that involved collisions and noise. When it was dry and sunny outside, we had endless options. We would ride escalators at our local mall, throw pennies into the wishing-well-fountain there, play in the park, do train rides on the little Griffith Park train, ride on merry-go-rounds, do picnics, feed ducks, eat ice cream, play games and whatever else Johnny wanted to do. We never just sat! Creativity was emerging under the influence of imagination.

As the weeks went by after the move, Johnny began to make friends with the neighbors, with the kids at his new church, with people of all stages of life, for age was not a barrier for him. He had a remarkable ability of quickly making connections with people because of his ready humor and zest for life. Like Curious George, the hero of the children's book series who consistently hurled himself into a new situation that had a daredevilish component to it, Johnny saw no limitations. He and Curious George were matchmates in audacious acts and in their natural curiosity of seeking to know the "why", the "what", the "when", the "how" questions of life. Alison mentioned this similarity often during Johnny's younger years.

Even as a baby, action had defined life with him. He had little interest in sleeping or napping. When he was just five months old, I can remember lying on the floor side by side with him and together doing bicycle leg exercises in the air. He would watch

Chapter 2

me exercise and then he would lift his little legs up in mimicking. Soon there were the days of crawling through plastic tunnels on our hands and knees, see-sawing and swinging, shooting basketballs into hoops of all sizes, and on and on. As I got older, there were times when I would get down on the floor to play, then struggle to get up when game time was over. Invariably, Johnny would offer his little hand, extend it towards mine, and say, "Mimi, I'll help you". He was so little and I was so big; it was truly touching to me.

One day when we were outdoors, he spotted a hopscotch game chalked out on a school play yard and he said to me, "Let's play that." I was then about seventy years old and jumping repetitively on one foot was way out of my league. But Johnny didn't know that and because he thought I could do it, I had to try. It turned into an hilarious game for both of us – fortunately no broken bones for me. It wasn't long before Johnny began challenging me to play football with him - then basketball. It was almost unbelievable that in his young mind, he saw me as able to do such feats, at least well enough for him to have some fun! Of course, he knew he would always be the winner! For me, it was a slingshot back into my youth. I longed to be able to demonstrate enough skill in these challenges to, with precision, give him a hearty game. I actually worked at visualizing myself as not only a viable ball player, but an accomplished one as well, hoping that the vision in my head would translate into reality. It didn't seem to improve my play at all. Johnny must have felt disappointment or frustration with my lack of accomplishments, but he didn't show it. He kept on with the challenges and the demonstrations of techniques. For a young boy, he showed surprising patience as a teacher. He was a natural athlete who seemed to have a desire to see others succeed. I loved that about him; I found myself thinking that perhaps when he grew up, he would become a physical education teacher, a coach, an athletic director. But that was his to decide. The world was wide open before him and his heart was full of dreams yet to be realized.

Chapter 3

SPUNK AND CHARACTER

"Whatever your hand finds to do, do it with all your might."
Ecclesiastes 9:10

Life in California was in full swing with Christopher and Emily in school and Johnny in preschool. He had waited four years for his turn to go to school; finally it had happened. Explosive enthusiasm sent him catapulting into the classroom three mornings a week. He enjoyed his teachers, his table mates, his crafts and projects. He loved to learn, yet he could hardly wait to get to the outdoor play times. The play yard was colorful and enticing. He could, with great spirit, run, slide, jump and have fun on all of the well-designed play equipment.

On Friday, May 12, 2006, an article appeared on the front page of the Santa Clarita edition of THE DAILY NEWS. The article was entitled, "Family Relies on Faith". The caption under the picture of Alison and Johnny read, "4-year-old boy fights battle against Cystic Fibrosis". The writer's lead paragraph said, "Johnny Buchanan, a tow-headed 4-year-old who bounces rather than walks, displays boundless energy that belies the traditional image of a youngster with Cystic Fibrosis". In just one brief interview, this journalist had captured the essence of Johnny. The uniqueness of his zest for life was constantly being communicated to others. His unbridled joy, his indomitable spirit, his spunk and overflowing enthusiasm for "living in the moment" all contributed to the unspoken creed that he lived by. Though he was too young to really understand the nature and ramifications of Cystic Fibrosis, he seemed to instinctively realize that he wasn't going to let his life be defined by something called Cystic Fibrosis. So much of the credit for his overcoming attitude about life is due not only to the lack of physical restrictions imposed upon Johnny by his parents, but to their positive mindset and optimism. Yes, he happens to have a condition called Cystic Fibrosis, but that is not who he is! He's their third-born, the precious son that God gifted to them, knowing that they were the kind of wise parents who could handle the challenges of CF because of who they were as people, as parents, and because of their deep faith in and reliance upon the God who created them all.

Life without his treatment regime was foreign to Johnny. Even as a two-year-old, he had intense tenacity and a spirit of entering into life fully, regardless of the difficulties presented. Occasionally, he would have to go into the hospital for what is commonly termed a "tune-up". As he became older, Johnny preferred to call it a "power boost". In his early years, he would pack up his mini doctor's kit with stethoscope, thermometer, band-aids and head out the door to the car with his spider-man suitcase rolling along in tow. On most of those occasions I would go along with Johnny and Alison. This was not only helpful to Alison; it also afforded me the opportunity to become well acquainted with Johnny's world in relation to CF. It's been a strong bond between the three of us. I observed what they went through - what took place at Children's Hospital. It didn't have to be explained. It was shared. I marveled during the span of those years to see how Alison was always prepared with her "treasure chest" of creative supplies and treats, thus enabling the clinic visits to be an adventure as well as a companionship time with mom and son. I also began to see glimpses of grit and courage in Johnny as he faced some of the procedures required in the clinic visits and hospital stays.

Chapter 3

Some were unpleasant and would have been frightful for adults to deal with. As a young lad, Johnny didn't like the blood draws in the lab, of course, or having to have surgical procedures for insertion of picc lines. They were traumatic for him, but over the years, he learned how to handle such protocol. He became a brave trooper.

Whenever he had to be hospitalized, Alison stayed in the room with him for the duration of his hospitalization, ranging anywhere from one to two weeks, being his advocate and helping him feel secure and safe. They were going through this whole thing together. Mike would be there, too, at times, to keep both Johnny and Alison company. Alison's diligence in helping Johnny become thoroughly acquainted with the rigors and necessities of following the daily treatments regime was a strong force in his eventual taking over the management of his health, I believe. She led the way with him, teaching him the vital importance of the time investment required for optimal results. Her optimistic approach was transmitted to Johnny as he learned from his parents that CF did not need to define who he was, as long as he did his part. He learned that he had to discipline himself to doing the full treatment regime every day, even when he didn't want to, and there were numerous times when that meant eliminating some play hours daily.

One of our habits right before leaving the hospital clinic was to go to the McDonalds located within the hospital for lunch, then to the Lollipop Store which is actually the Hospital Gift Shop. It's filled with a variety of candies and sweet treats as well as stuffed animals, toys and games – and of course, colorful, tasty lollipops. The Lollipop Store continued to be a favorite part of the trips to see the doctor for many years. By the time he was seven or eight, Johnny had become fascinated with riding the hospital elevator to the seventh floor where he could get the best panoramic view of the famous Hollywood Sign. He often talked about going to see the sign up close one day. As the years went by, visits to McDonalds and the Lollipop Store were replaced by more grown-up lunches at Panda Express and a favored Yogurtland dessert - side-by-side eateries right on the way home from the clinic. Perhaps Johnny had spotted them from the seventh floor view!

    My mind sometimes thinks of the day at Children's Hospital, LA, when Alison, Johnny and I were hurrying to catch the elevator. In my haste, I managed to slip on some wet orchid petals on the floor in the lobby of the hospital. I took a hard fall, face down, and ended up with a scraped, bleeding knee. I couldn't get up! Lying on the terrazzo floor, I heard the voice of a nearby hospital security guard asking me if I would like a wheelchair. Johnny, who was right beside me, politely spoke up and said, "she doesn't need a wheelchair now. She needs to be helped up and given some band-aids for the bleeding." I had to laugh! Johnny's quick assessment of a situation and the resolution were at work again. It was as though he, in trying to assure me, had said, "Don't worry, Mimi. I got this!" He was probably ten or eleven at the time. On the ride home from the hospital, I told him that his Aunt Jeanie and I had just been talking about bad falls we each had taken. Johnny's quick comment was, "maybe you and Aunt Jeanie in your next conversation should talk about winning the lottery." He's nailed it again, I thought.

CHAPTER 4

IN THE MOMENT

"Be ready in season and out of season."
2 Timothy 4:2

It was summertime in Southern California! We had special plans for the day – plans with the Buchanan kids. Such days were always eventful, full of surprises of spontaneous encounters. We had found it to be so throughout the years whenever we were engaged in an activity with any of our grandchildren, most of whom were teen-agers now – fascinating, full of fun and thoroughly refreshing to be with. It delighted us that they still liked doing things with us! Perhaps that's because we'd shared lives since they were only babies.

On this particular day we were taking Christopher, Emily and Johnny to a matinee of the film, "A Shark's Tale". The kids were ready to go when we arrived. Christopher and Emily raced out to the car. Johnny, who was four at the time, came bounding down the stairs, and when we saw him, we could hardly keep from laughing. He was dressed in a bright yellow T-shirt sporting a picture of an enormous shark on the front. The T-shirt hung almost to his knees. Covering his eyes were his swim goggles and in his hands were his swim fins. He was "into the moment" and ready to see A Shark's Tale.

As we walked from the car park towards the theater, Johnny seemed impervious to the stares of passer-byers who obviously had noticed his attire. He was too busy bouncing and telling stories to notice the actions of others. In his very animated, voluminous voice, he had constant streams of stories to tell. At the theater, the ticket collector smiled broadly when he saw him. He gave a "thumbs up", a "high-five" to him, and remarked, "I like your spirit. You're good to go, young man." During the film, Johnny did remove his goggles, and we put the fins in my tote bag when we hauled out the Shark's Fin Fruit Snacks, and in between bathroom trips, and back to the popcorn counter for more butter on the corn, we all thoroughly enjoyed the film. Perhaps Johnny had enjoyed it most of all, for he had entered into it with complete wholeheartedness. When he would help his daddy with repairs, he'd run to get his own little plastic tool kit, which held an assortment of screwdrivers, various wrenches and even a tape measure and hammer (plus a few little boy's treasures). To help his mom in the kitchen, which was anytime he wasn't occupied in any other activity, he'd dash off to another room to fetch a stool and lug it back to the kitchen counter so that he could stand tall enough to break the eggshells, or spread the jam. Time and again when his brother, Christopher, would be scheduled for a soccer or football game, Johnny would be the first one in the family ready to go out the door, dressed in team attire, carrying a ball appropriate for the sport of the day. He had the vision of being a player in life – not a spectator, and from head to toe, he took the steps to make it happen. Being fully engaged in the moment is a magnetic characteristic of Johnny, one which has given us insight and inspiration into new ways of doing things in our own lives.

    Christopher and Emily were students at Trinity Classical Academy in Santa Clarita. Johnny entered Trinity as a first-grader. He'd been at Trinity for only a few months when he found himself in a conflict between enjoying the social aspect of the

Chapter 4

school, but frustrated by the academic demands required. The difficulty came in pages of daily homework; he found this to be irritating, time-consuming; it was cutting into his play time. One day after struggling with the homework, he said to his Mom, who was helping him with it all, "I'm tired of this. I'm quitting." Alison wisely told him that quitting wasn't an option. She said, "we don't quit when things get hard; we take breaks, and then get back to what we have to do and keep going." Several weeks later, Alison heard him mumbling under his breath, "I quit CF, I quit CF." He was tired of the continual breathing therapy which also interfered with outdoor activities. Soon enough he returned to his normal pattern of tackling both his homework and his CF chest treatments. Neither his logical mind nor his spirit would allow him to bail out.

Chapter 5
JOHNNY JOY

*"He who is of a merry heart has a continual feast.
Life is a banquet when one is joyful".*
Proverbs 15:15

My heart was immersed in sadness one day because Johnny was ill. We, in our family, were so accustomed to his buoyancy of spirit and fun antics but now he was still and quiet on his bed, very gray of color, very listless. The world can seem quite bleak when you have a loved one who is ill. I was frightened and experiencing a turbulent churning in the pit of my stomach. His symptoms were indicative of a viral infection or a seasonal flu. Because it was a Saturday and doctor's offices were closed, Johnny was riding out the week-end, with high hopes by all of us that he would be much better on Monday. Whatever it was, it had hit with a vengeance.

As I thought about the contrast between the wellness of Johnny and the sickness of Johnny, I was reminded of the stark contrast between day and night. In the daytime we have the energy, the warmth of the sun, the brightness of the light, the capacity to see distinctly and the clarity and safety that this provides. We're able to experience the brilliance and beauty of God's creation, and the visible security of the world that we know. The nighttime is dark, oft times cold, ominous, filled with the unknown; imaginations can so easily run amiss. It is easy to feel afraid, insecure. I was wondering if Johnny had experienced these things in his unexpected encounter with sickness and the accompanying disturbance to his whole

Chapter 5

body. His world was a departure from the norm; he clung to the most loving security that he knew – his mom, his dad, his family.

Several days had passed and he seemed somewhat improved. Bob and I had decided to go to the store to buy a colorful bouquet of balloons to help cheer him up, along with an activity book and a pair of SpongeBob pajamas. How happy we were to see his face break into a smile when we walked in with our surprises! It meant the world to me to see some of his spark returning. The heavy feeling in the pit of my stomach was replaced by "Johnny Joy". How good it was again to feel that way. It was like passing through the brooding clouds of a turbulent storm to the spectacular brightness of a rainbow when the sun blazes forth after a rainstorm. It's a moment in time that is captivating to your soul and spirit, and you want to relish it and live there for a bit! You feel wrapped up in the rainbow – it's warmth, it's completeness of color, its hug of gladness. Alison remembered that when the children were younger and rather "down" about something, she and Mike would say to the kids, "You need a Johnny smile." Johnny was only a baby then but when they could elicit a smile from him, it cheered them up.

Milestones given worth by others aren't always as memorable in a life as the small moments of tender times together; those become the truly triumphant mountain peaks. This had been such a moment for me – the triumph of Johnny's returning to health again. Throughout the coming years, there would be other such times – times of sickness and returns to health. But this particular time that I've described stands out as forever embedded in my heart. I so clearly remembered praying passionately that God would give His angels charge over Johnny to protect him from harm, asking that God's healing hand would cover every part of Johnny's body with health and wholeness. I prayed for peace for Johnny and his parents and for all of us who loved him so much. God, in His Goodness, answered our prayers for healing and our hearts bowed before Him in thanksgiving and in joy.

After he was completely well, Johnny, in his rather dramatic way, commented to his Mom, "I can't believe that I didn't die when I was sick." His unspoken concern had been his bedfellow and now he was well and able to express his feelings in his usual open book manner. It's a refreshing characteristic of his!

Forever lodged in my heart, is a time of Johnny Joy that happened when he was ten or eleven. In this particular year, he had been hospitalized in early December for about a week. He was discharged just prior to Christmas and was filled with such delight to be home that he wasted no time in digging out some Christmas decorations; immediately he began to decorate the upstairs hall that connected all four bedrooms of his house. He took long strings of red lights and in a script fashion, spelled out the word "JOY". The span of it probably covered about eight feet or so. He then took strings of multi-colored lights and decorated each of the four bedroom door frames as well as around bathroom mirrors. It looked beautiful; so alive with anticipation of the Christmas season. Within the next few days, after working with his dad on outdoor lights for their home, he came across the street to our house to help with our decorations. He and his Papa spent many hours making our front yard and porch look merry and bright with candy cane lights bordering the front lawn and the approach to the front door, also trimming the porch and eaves. Knowing Johnny as well as I did, I was still astonished by the depth of his expression of what it meant to be joyfully alive and living in the moment. It was as though the discharge of all of the pent-up week in the hospital caused an explosion of virtual joy that saturated his being and was released in immediately entering into the festivities of the Christmas season. His celebration had been launched.

Johnny's joy and sense of humor are prevalent. He loves to tease; it's not always been easy to discern whether he's jesting or serious. Pranks, riddles, jokes; all are right up his alley. One of the antics that used to elicit laughter was his sudden, dramatic appearance in some sort of avante garde costume; capes, boots, zany hats, swords, sashes, masks. We never knew who would be coming down the stairs, dashing into the room. Yet, with all of his merriment, there is a sensitive side to him that is quite tender. Early in the morning one day he telephoned. In a very solemn tone he said, "Mimi, I have some sad news." When I asked him about it, he told me that he had just heard on a television news report that the crooked-neck giraffe at the Santa Barbara Zoo had died. We had been to see the giraffe several times and Johnny had been fascinated in watching him move so gracefully, eating leaves from the tall trees of his habitat. You couldn't help but marvel as you watched him combat the challenges of his life. Interestingly enough, several hours after Johnny's phone call, my then seventeen year old grandson called with the same sad news. He, too, has a sensitive spirit. He, too, had been to see the giraffe. I like to think that because of the unusualness of this particular giraffe and the stalwart way in which he had to live his life, that he had captured the hearts of people of all ages and that we were all united in honoring him, recognizing in him a champion's spirit.

CHAPTER 6

A BOY AND A BALL

"And a little child shall lead them."
Isaiah 11:6

Johnny and a ball had become inseparable. It's almost as though he and a ball moved as one. He had said to me that "a ball is everything". So often when I would see him, he would be engaged in bouncing some type of a ball. Usually it would be a basketball; sometimes a volleyball, soccer ball, tennis ball, - just any kind of ball would do, as long as it was round and bounced, or oval and could be thrown. Not surprisingly he lived and breathed to play sports. In 2010, he was quarterback of his flag football team; also captain of his basketball team. He played soccer as well. His trophies took up two rows of shelves on the wall of his bedroom. When he attended his brother's varsity basketball games, he could hardly wait until half-time, when he would grab the moment to take his ball to the gym floor to shoot baskets. He was poised and waiting for an opportunity to do some shooting, even during those brief moments when a time-out would be called.

He served as the ball boy for the Trinity High School Varsity football team during the years that Christopher played on the team. Johnny loved being a part of the whole scenario. One of his heroes on the team (other than his brother) was James, a 6 foot 5 inch outstanding athlete and Johnny's personal friend. You could almost always find Johnny hanging around James on a ball field - be it football, basketball, or baseball. James's football jersey bore the number "2". When

Chapter 6

Johnny was hospitalized in November of 2011 and had to miss the last football game of the season, the high school boys on the team had a special jersey made just for him, with the number "2" on it. It was presented to him in the hospital, along with a football that some of the players had signed. It was a high moment in the life of a ten-year old boy who had a passion for not only playing ball, but also for being "one of the guys on the team".

On one occasion, we were sitting at a Trinity Varsity baseball game. Normally at such games, Johnny served as the unofficial ball chaser. He expended great energy in retrieving foul balls that would fly outside of the field perimeter and in returning the balls to the dugout. On this particular day, he had winsomely ended up in the scorekeeper's booth, eating sunflower seeds, and posting data on the electric scoreboard. Of course, his mom and his Papa Keith were in the score booth with him for corroboration as official scorekeepers. From his vantage point on a bleacher bench, Papa Bob had humorously remarked that if you opened the door just a crack, Johnny would stride on through and make himself invaluable. After the ball game had concluded, he was out on the field, brushing down the diamond with the team. In his strong desire to always want to be a part of whatever was happening, he had learned to do a great many things that would serve him well in life, and in joining right in with an activity, he had proven himself to be a valuable contributor, if not indispensable!

Background work in the film industry captured the interest of all three of the Buchanan kids for several years. Los Angeles was, and still is, a mecca for opportunities in film work in both television and movies. "Only in Hollywood!" But no, set locations were all over greater Los Angeles as well as outlying areas. We learned that parents and their minor aged children would travel from surrounding states and relocate in Southern California on a temporary basis to take the casting calls for a chance at being a part of a production. Casting calls would often come in the evenings prior to a need to be on location the next day. The people who frequently responded affirmatively were the ones the studios would consistently call upon to work. Shooting sites could be anywhere from crowded, downtown locations, to outlying suburbs, to remote ranches reached by dirt road travel. The hours on location might be as long as eight. In such cases it was necessary that several of the hours be set aside as school time for homework purposes with a supervising teacher on site in order to comply with the requirements of the child labor laws. Food was provided by the studio and served on location; breakfast, lunch, dinner or snacks depending on the number of hours worked. Wardrobe selection could be needed; more generally items were brought from home. If not approved by wardrobe personnel, apparel was available on site. Adrenalin flowed freely in the process of arising early in the morning, hustling to battle traffic to travel to a heretofore unknown destination to arrive on time. Studio promptness was mandatory! For a mid- afternoon or evening casting call, it might be as late as midnight before you would arrive home.

    At times, rehearsals would take hours of doing repetitive shoots. Johnny initially enjoyed the life of an occasional background film guy, so much so that he chose to pursue auditioning for speaking roles. He acquired a manager, an agent and took acting lessons, but waiting for calls to audition was time consuming and Johnny eventually lost interest. He decided that there wasn't enough action for him. He was getting into the world of team sports at school and as a team player, he believed in never missing a practice or a game if at all possible.

Sports play became a priority and the film work faded into the past! It had been a rewarding experience, but he had decided that it was time for it to end.

One day when Johnny was about nine or so, we watched a few plays of a football game on the television set at his house. I noticed that the football players were wearing pink socks - in recognition of Breast Cancer Awareness month. I mentioned to him that I had a friend who had cancer. He asked where her cancer was. I told him it was a cancer of the bones. Immediately he ran to get a Bible and then read a passage to me from Psalm 6:2: "Have mercy on me, O Lord, for I am weak; O Lord, heal me, for my bones are troubled." Johnny had heard the verse that morning in a Sunday School class, and not only did he remember it; he made a practical application of it to a real life situation. I was deeply impressed with his spiritual maturity; I wrote a note to my friend who was battling cancer of the bones and shared this story with her. She was touched by Johnny's concern and his faith that knew and believed in God's Word.

A "boy and a ball" - these were a portrait of Johnny's life as a youngster, a portrait that would capture the essence of his high school years at an even more core level. The best was yet to come!

CHAPTER 7

BEARS, PENGUINS & GUMMY WORMS

"Rejoice young man in your youth and let your heart cheer you in the days of your youth."
Ecclesiastes 11:9

The story within this chapter triggers "the kid still within us all," which hopefully will never entirely depart. We were in the midst of The Build-A-Bear phenomenon, which was soaring. All across the large cities of America, children and parents were flocking to Build-A-Bear stores to buy stuffed bears and all manner of custom clothing to dress the bears. The bears were honey colored, dark brown, panda or white and upon purchasing one, it would be put into a fluffing machine to fill it up and out in order to make the bear nicely plump. Imaginative designers had fabricated spunky, snappy, clothing for the bears. Shorts, pants, shirts, suits, ties, dresses, skirts, costumes, sports outfits, military garb, graduation gowns, beach attire, shoes, boots, sandals, skateboards, sunglasses and all of the accessories for dress-up lined the shelves and bins. Tigers, puppy dogs, kittens and other animal choices were also available. The clothing was designed to fit any of the animals sold there. Build-A-Bear birthday parties were the rage. It was a uniquely designed business!

Emily and Johnny were young enough to be fascinated with the bears and their clothing. For several years, Bob and I and the kids made trips to the Build-A-Bear store, then home to dress the bears in their new clothing and do "let's pretend" stories

Chapter 7

and dramas with the bears. When Aunt Jeanie (my sister) would come to town, we'd have bear tea parties or picnics in our dining room. The table would be dressed festively, laden with kid-friendly foods. Pizza triangles, carrot sticks, apple slices, chips, cantaloupe balls and grapes, honey cookies, Hershey kisses, lemonade - these were favorites with the kids, the bears and the grown-ups. The bears would sit in their own chairs, propped up high on pillows in order to reach the food and eat to their heart's content. The children have photos of such occasions. Johnny and Emily loved those times. We did, too!

The bears, as fascinating as they were, never really competed in Johnny's heart with Snowball, his soft, stuffed penguin. Snowball was his bed buddy for many years, always accompanying him to Children's Hospital or on vacation trips. Snowball often traveled in "the little tin suitcase" - a small metallic-like travel case that Johnny through the years dubbed "the little tin suitcase". To this day, it is still being used by him and other family members. Snowball's many travels led to numerous machine washings which left him with a rather ragged, aged look. That didn't affect his lovability at all in Johnny's eyes.

Through the years, whenever Aunt Jeanie would come for a visit, the kids would begin to prepare for her arrival by making an assortment of welcome signs, banners, posters – colorful drawings. We would hang these all around the house in places of high visibility. Johnny would brace himself to expect to hear frequently one of Aunt Jeanie's favorite phrases to him, "Johnny, wash your hands." Over the years, it did help him in developing that habit, and he never seemed to mind her yearly reminders. One year, Johnny challenged Aunt Jeanie and me to play in a basketball tournament with him. He typed up a list of the tournament games including the rules regulating each one. This list was posted in a prominent place in our house so that we saw it daily. Jeanie and I, with all of the zest that we could muster, hurled ourselves into gaining an Olympian mentality to compete as triumphant victors. The day of the tournament finally arrived; tension was mounting. Johnny's outdoor curbside basketball stand in front of his house had been lowered to less than regulation height in order to accommodate the senior competition. A court had been chalked out. It was a warm Sunday afternoon and some of the neighborhood children had gathered to watch. Alison and Mike were in the audience as well, along with Papa who was taking pictures of the long-awaited event. Aunt Jeanie and I (our combined ages totaled 152 years) were feeling a bit foolish to be on neighborhood display, but we were determined to play the game of our lives. We had dressed in matching Kermit the Frog T-shirts since we were "Team Kermit." Our official mascot, a long-legged large stuffed Kermit, proudly sat on a tall director's chair near the court to cheer us on. Jeanie and I were comical; Johnny a skilled athlete. He bounced onto the court, carrying his ball, dressed in navy and gray, looking like a true basketball player – which he was. A prize and the title; these were the spoils. Our game lasted for about an hour and in the end Team Kermit played much better than anyone had expected (including Johnny) thanks to Aunt Jeanie's "around the world" game skills. Johnny was the overall winner of the tournament though and triumphantly, but graciously, with his face sweaty and hot, and beaming with smiles, he accepted his prizes and applause. Aunt Jeanie and I staggered home to collapse on the nearest sofas. Our prizes lay in the successful completion of the game and in still being alive to tell the tale!

Chapter 7

During Jeanie's visits, we would hold a different competition each year. In the year pursuant to the basketball challenge, we had competed in a rousing game of neon miniature golf. Another year we held a tournament in our back yard, competing in ladder ball and croquet. One year, we designed a challenge of making escalating pyramids of tall and intricately wide towers from disposable plastic tumblers, with the objective being to have your tower be the last one standing. It became apparent that whatever the competition event was, when Johnny felt secure in his position as the victor, he would come to the rescue of the underdog to help in her quest for second place. Jeanie and I also noticed that after the great basketball challenge spectacle, each succeeding competition had been created by Johnny to be less physically exerting on us. His innate kindness was being demonstrated. Finally, we were reduced to two sisters whose challenge was so minimal that Johnny humorously made the statement, "next year when Aunt Jeanie comes, we might have to play board games for our competition." Not really dynamic enough from his perspective!

Most of my stories of Johnny revolve around his mindset of stepping into the world of creativity. I found his thinking outside of the box to be fascinating, often pondering "what next!" He was bold in trying to concoct new recipes, as well as generous in sharing his bounty with me. One of his favorite snacks was Maraschino cherries, which were as prevalent on our refrigerator shelves as milk and eggs. He decorated numerous foods with them, devouring them by the jar. I'm sure he must have returned home with a shirt streaked with cherry juice. But without question, Johnny's all-time favorite snack from kindergarten through high school days were gummy worms. Hundreds of bags were purchased for gifts to him throughout those years. Had we only invested in Gummy Worm stock, we'd be in our dream beach homes now!

Several years ago, the five Buchanans and Bob and I spent a day at Disneyland. The magic of Disneyland - it had drawn us there time and time again over the years. Some of our older grandchildren continued to love it as we did. Through the years, we would take any of the grandkids who wanted to go on an annual trip to The Magic Kingdom – always during the first week in December when it would be less crowded than closer to Christmas. The Park was then exquisitely dressed for the holidays. To us, those days with our pre-teen and teen aged grandsons were highlights of the Christmas season, not only for the pure joy of exploring the Park with them at its most festive time of the year, but also we found it to be releasing in our own hearts the fun of being kids again in the sense of leaving the stress of the busyness of the season behind and getting away to enjoy a play day!

On this particular day, we had covered Tomorrowland, Adventureland, and were in Frontierland when hunger struck. Off we went to see the show and eat at the Golden Horseshoe Saloon which had delicious chili/cheese fries and fancy waffle ice cream dishes. The show was about ready to start when we arrived. The entertainment was a rowdy hillbilly satire. The main character in the skit had sinister-looking eyes, and missing front teeth. The remaining ones were yellow-stained and broken. He spoke in a repugnantly loud, overbearing manner. We had a table close to the stage and Hillbilly Bill loomed larger than life directly in front of us as he performed. After listening to him for a few moments, Johnny made it clear that he didn't like this show at all. His first comment was, "I'll never bring my child here." Johnny was eight at the time! After it was finally over,

Chapter 7

he exclaimed so seriously, "I wish they'd had technical difficulties so the show couldn't have gone on." I don't believe he's been back to the Golden Horseshoe since.

Christmas day of 2011 had arrived. Our entire family was celebrating the day in our home. Johnny's top wish for Christmas was for a surfboard. He'd talked about it for months. His Aunt Linda, Uncle Bob and cousin, Casey, were giving him one. It was hidden in our garage, adorned with an enormous red bow with streamers that went the length of the surfboard. Bob and I had decided to give him a wetsuit to go with the surfboard. The wetsuit was the final present he opened that afternoon. At this point, but unknown to Johnny, his Christmas surfboard was floating in our swimming pool. Johnny was summoned outside by someone in the family, and when he spotted the ribbon-decorated surfboard in the pool, he let out a stream of cheers that could have broken the sound barrier. Immediately, he ran back into the house, donned his new wetsuit and splashed into the cold December water to climb aboard his new gift. No surf - no waves, but he didn't care. He was riding high!

CHAPTER 8

DOUBLE DIGITS

"Let no one not respect your youth, but be an example to the believers in word, in conduct, in love, in spirit, in faith, in purity."
1 Timothy 4:12

Johnny was close to turning ten years old! This would be a coming of age event – his entrance into the world of "double digits". Parties for both his friends and his family were being planned, his "wish list" was on the computer, and there was an air of excitement in the family as we talked about ideas and surprises that we hoped would make for a memorable celebration for him. Needless to say, he was over the top with excitement and it seemed as though "THE BIG EVENT" was taking on a life of its own. I think this was so because we felt immense joy in seeing this day come, not only to the youngest grandchild in the family of the Augur clan, but to one who had battled persistent health issues so triumphantly. He had always loved celebrating any event, throwing himself into it with balloons, signs, posters and whatever clothing he saw as befitting the occasion. We desired to do the same for him.

Johnny had designed his friends' party to be in our backyard and swimming pool area. The dozen or so kids that came included his special friends from elementary school days. Greg was one. He and Johnny couldn't have been more different. Greg would come to the house and sit inside, playing some of the early video games that peaked his interest. Johnny would be outside, playing active games with like-minded neighbor friends. Interestingly enough, Johnny and Greg continue in friendship as

Chapter 8

collegiates; Greg is a UCBerkley student, studying mechanical engineering, and Johnny is playing University volleyball as a Biblical Studies major. The two have enjoyed hiking together all through the years. The kids at the party had a ton of fun with competitive games: oiled watermelons to lift out of the pool and roll in a distance race, crawl races to paper plates filled with swirls of whipped cream to bury your face in and other creative antics. The party was a huge success, just what we had all hoped for!

From babies to seniors, Johnny has had a magnetic connection with people. One evening we had a group of friends over for dinner. About five minutes after they arrived and their cars were parked in front of our home, which was very visible from the Buchanan home, our phone rang. Johnny was calling to see if it was alright if he came over to meet our friends. He liked being a part of things. He didn't stay long; he was working on a school project at home that was due the following morning. His fourth grade class was involved in a Reformation Day presentation. Johnny had been assigned the role of John Wycliffe the renowned Bible translator. As part of this assignment, he was to not only give a dramatic portrayal of the historic theologian, but also research and present a display board of information about John Wycliffe. He'd spent many hours on the project. After our friends left our home, the phone rang again. Johnny invited us to come to his house to see his completed work. He enthusiastically read to us all of the information he had garnered and displayed. He was proud of what he had accomplished, and his excitement about it was infectious. John Wycliffe took on much more of a "real life" to us because of a young boy's passion to portray him accurately and well.

In the backyard of our Bettina Court home, there was a

most unusual tree; a Ponderosa lemon tree. Its uniqueness lay in the enormous size of the lemons. Their girth could match that of a huge grapefruit. How disappointed we were when we first halved one and tried to squeeze juice from it. There was barely a trickle to extract and the few drops we managed to acquire were bitterly tart. Everything we tried to make from the lemons was totally unsuccessful so in the end, we switched gears and Johnny started using them for juggling practice. As a pre-teenager, he was becoming quite proficient in juggling. Tennis balls, oranges, apples, limes, Ponderosa lemons; almost anything of which there were three to six items - these were his to toss. Different sizes and weights were more challenging but more interesting to him. It was intriguing to watch, especially from my perspective of having no skill in such things. Along with juggling, he was interested in the world of magic – causing things to appear and disappear. Tricks with coins, cards, and handkerchiefs were performed almost daily. Card tricks were a favorite. His hand was indeed quicker than my eye. I loved watching his success in these ventures. If things were difficult for him, he didn't give up. He continued to try to be proficient, demonstrating an inner drive that spurred him onward.

One evening around dusk, the front screen door slammed and Johnny came barreling into the kitchen, short of breath, and yelling, "Mimi, Mimi do you have any graham crackers? The neighbors have their fire pit going and we want to make s'mores." I was so happy that we had a brand new box of the grahams and he practically cartwheeled out the front door before torpedoing down the street with the box in hand to join his cul-de-sac friends.

Such times were one of the soul-satisfying reasons why we loved living where we did. You can well imagine the delight we took in the daily connections we were able to make with our grandchildren in having playful fun as well as in enjoying the days of bridging the past and the present. To me, it was a grandparents' dream like no other. Sometimes, I would pinch myself and say, "Really, Lord Jesus, you're blessing us beyond belief. You are so very, very good to us."

Johnny had reached the age of eleven. It was a lovely fall day in November of 2012 in Southern California. Alison and Johnny were with us in Carlsbad, a beach town on the California coast. It was late in the afternoon when we made the short walk from the resort condo where we were staying to steps that would lead down to the warm sandy beach. Alison and Johnny tested the water and decided that it definitely was warm enough for a swim and some body surfing. Other people were nearby in the water.

I had taken a book and a beach chair with me intending to catch up on some reading while the others swam. But after reading for a bit, I looked up to see dozens, or so it seemed, of seagulls gathered in a flock on the sand about a hundred yards away from me. I was intrigued with watching them until my eyes looked beyond the gulls to see an extraordinary sight. Alison and Johnny were body surfing together, capsulated in what appeared to be the rays of a magnificent sunbeam. A sailing vessel was near the horizon. One lone seagull had departed from the flock to stand by the water's edge, looking to sea, as though a guardian of the surfers.

I was enthralled by the sight; it impressed itself upon my mind vividly. A caption flashed before me; a caption of "mother and son, play buddies, riding the sunbeam together." It was a moment in time that presented itself as a portrait of their relationship through the years – "play buddies" in many arenas of life. I savored watching it and being in the moment with them. There had been other beach times together in California as well as in Hawaii, but never had I seen a display of sunbeam brilliance enveloping my family. I'm not sure if they were cognizant of this masterpiece of God's unheralded gift or not. To me, it appeared to be almost sacred, something to harbor in my heart as though in speaking of it, it would cease to be real.

CHAPTER 9

THE REDEMPTION TREE

"So the child grew and became strong in spirit."
Luke 1:80

It was a Sunday afternoon in May. Alison, Emily and Johnny had carried a table and chair set to our garage to store for an upcoming garage sale. We talked for a while before Alison and Emily went home to take care of some things. Johnny stayed and hung out with me in the front yard – the same yard that had once "housed" a huge and lovely tree. Let me tell you the story of this tree. It begins with the purchase of our Bettina Court home in 2010 - a home that we were certain was presented to us by God because the timing was right for a move for us, and because the house was on a lovely cul-de-sac just across the street from the Buchanans. In the front yard, stood a beautiful weeping willow tree dominating the entire lawn. It was part of the charm of the home - the tree and the house together, providing not only beauty but welcoming shade on hot summer days.

However, the tree had internal problems and several arborists had declared it to be quite diseased; a disaster waiting to happen. We then came close to not buying the home. Our daughter-in-law, who was also our realtor and a dedicated Christian, wisely said to me, "Mom you're not going to let Satan rob you of that which God is presenting to you, are you?" As we thought about it, we realized that God was speaking to us through her and we proceeded in purchasing the house. We also chose not to have the tree removed, but to pray that the tree would stand and continue to provide shade and beauty. Little by little in the spring of the year, God pruned the tree with the windstorms that are prevalent in Castaic. He also spoke to my heart to say that "the tree would stand as long as He had use and purpose for it, just as we would." At that point, in our minds and hearts, we released concern over the tree. Peace replaced worry. In mid-October of the year while we were in Canada on vacation, Alison called to say that several of the huge, major branches on the tree had fallen due to a veracious windstorm. No one, no car, no part of our home nor our neighbors' homes had been damaged. We were left with a gigantic trunk from which three large barren truncated branches rose fifteen to twenty feet in the air. At Christmastime, we had decorated the truncated branches, though quite dead looking, with Christmas lights, red velvet bows and a large Bethlehem star on the tallest of the barren boughs. Neighbors and walkers were attracted to it and the comments were priceless. We had a positive mindset in regard to the changes that had occurred for several reasons; we were enjoying the openness this brought to the yard, we recognized God's timing in all of it and the miracle of His speaking into our lives, and we were cognizant of the testimony and "legacy of the tree" to our family. Surprisingly, in the spring of the year, we noticed green shoots sprouting from the central trunk of the tree. By Easter time the tree had been transformed into a tall, lovely umbrella of greenery, more beautiful and fitting for the yard than the original shape when we purchased the house. I write of this because I believe that it's important to note that though this was just a tree, it became much more than a tree. God had spoken directly, prophetically into our lives. He Illustrated so vividly and personally to us that He can change the ordinary into the extraordinary. Indeed He had, and so it is with all of us when He's directing our actions and our lives.

    Johnny liked to sit under the new shoots. He had the

Chapter 9

idea that it would be fun to sit under "The Redemption Tree" – his name for it, on a hot summer day and eat popsicles. Emily saw it as a reader or writer's paradise. Near The Redemption Tree was a pretty little corner garden with some rose bushes, a bed of green moss, and a tall, Madagascar palm tree. Johnny was intrigued by the bed of green moss underneath and all around it, being captured by its softness. He wanted to transplant it to the ground underneath The Redemption Tree and then lie down on it.

Don't you love the vision of a young boy of ten lying on a soft green mossy bed under an umbrella of green branches allowing for filtered sunlight, chewing on a blade of grass, looking up at the sky, seeing fanciful shapes in the clouds, dreaming dreams, thinking thoughts - and being still for just a moment to enjoy God's beautiful creation. "The Lord is my Shepherd, I shall not want. He makes me to lie down in green pasture. He restores my soul." (Psalm 23: 1-2)

The Redemption Tree spoke to me of "The Cross, the Cross of Jesus." One day when Johnny had some free time, he discovered some old, used 2x4 scraps of wood in his garage – not sanded but rough in texture. He took a hammer, a saw, some nails and fashioned two large four-foot crosses. He and his dad staked one of the crosses in their yard. We commented on it several times. Not long afterwards, Johnny carried a cross to our house and asked if we would like to have it. Delight filled my heart to have a cross that Johnny had made. He helped us settle it into a dirt bed that flanked our backyard swimming pool. There were green plants and ground cover on either side of it, which set the cross off beautifully. It was placed in such a position that from the windows in our family room and kitchen, even from the front door, we could easily see it. That year our

Christmas card greeting was a picture of Johnny's cross with vibrant red poinsettias at its base. When we moved to another house several years later, we took the weathered cross with us and today it stands in our backyard, near the swimming pool, very visible from inside our home. It's quite meaningful to us to see the cross in the foreground behind our home. It brings love-filled memories and a resting peace, even as it speaks of life. "The Old Rugged Cross" – a timeless hymn sung in churches across America resounds in my heart at times when my focus is directed to our backyard cross. As a young girl growing up, living for a time with my grandmother and attending her church, we often sang that hymn and the lyrics would flood through my soul once again. A view of the cross in the early dawn of a morning when the sunrise is brilliantly spreading across the eastern sky, forming a backdrop for the silhouette of the cross, is one of the most emotionally moving sights of my lifetime. The sheer beauty of this extraordinary display of God's majestic handiwork is breath-taking. In my heart I am taken again and again to the foot of the cross in humbling adoration of our Lord Jesus, who, in love, gave His all that we might live. Never has there been a comparable sacrifice.

CHAPTER 10
THE SOUND OF THE SCOOTER

"Blessed are the people who know the joyful sound."
Psalm 89:15

Johnny and his scooter were a familiar sight in our cul-de-sac neighborhood of Bettina Court as he traveled the short distance between his house and houses of neighborhood friends. He also had another traveling vehicle – the green machine cycle that he used to buzz around the cul-de-sac to Cassie and Katie's or Nick's houses. It was fun to ride, he said, though more cumbersome and not as fast as the scooter could be. During his home schooling years, he often rode his scooter to our house. Recognizing his need for a school break, Alison would give him permission to come to our house for brief periods throughout the day. He would set his wrist watch alarm for 20 or 30 minutes and off he'd come. His scooter, though sleek of appearance with its silver coating, had a loud, distinctive rattle that hallmarked its imminent arrival. Knowing that the scooter would momentarily be parked on our little front porch and Johnny would come bursting through the door, I quickly would put aside whatever I was doing in order to be available for him. Our kitchen cupboards and refrigerator were well stocked with his favorite items for often his visits had to do with food hopes - maraschino cherries, fresh mushrooms to saute, quesadillas, cool-whip topped items. I treasured the brief interludes when Johnny would come to spend some time with me, knowing that such moments wouldn't last forever. Sometimes we'd play games or do riddles, talk or cook and eat or plan competition games for the days each winter when Aunt Jeanie would arrive for a visit.

He frequently used his scooter as a means of transporting items from our house to his. It was not at all unusual to see him load up the handlebars with plastic bags containing gallon milk cartons, eggs, cheeses, grapes or baking potatoes and ride home with his treasures - a smile on his face and a happy heart. I would soon run off to the grocery store to restock to be ready for the next visit.

I discovered that, at times, when in the mood, Johnny enjoyed cooking. He actually was an innovative, budding chef. On one occasion, in our home, he made an unbelievably tasty breakfast for Jeanie and me in preparing something we'd never had before; poached eggs served in a warm ripe avocado half. It was presented looking like a creation out of Gourmet Delights. How delicious it was! When I needed to make about two hundred lemon bars for a family wedding, Johnny was in my kitchen day after day to help bake, cut and arrange the bars in small paper pastry cups. It was a true labor of love on his part; however, in the end we agreed that our lemon bar baking careers had ceased! We had reached a saturation point. On another occasion, Johnny came to my rescue when I decided one year to make an assortment of Italian dishes for Christmas Day dinner for about twenty people. He worked right alongside of me in the making of Italian Wedding Soup, a dish that neither of us had ever tasted or prepared. It required the forming of countless small, seasoned ground chicken meatballs. Upon tasting the soup, we decided that next time, we'd make a few changes. Next time came once, but never after that. We sometimes made a dish of spinach-stuffed pasta shells. His part came in stuffing the spinach/creamed cheeses mixture into the jumbo shells – a time consuming task. He liked eating the finished product, so he never seemed to mind the tedious preparation. Often when I would be making what we call Augur Burgers, he would help in the formation of the large ground chuck patties which then needed to be patted into a rather flat shape of filling the hamburger bun halves headed for the oven to bake. He enjoyed the vigorous patting down – more like "slapping", of the meat onto the bun!

The true gifts of Johnny's visits were a rooted anchoring of the love and companionship that had been established in his infancy – a relationship that God continually allowed us to enjoy in his growing-up years. I marveled, and still do, that a young boy would find an aging grandmother to be an adequate playmate – someone he liked to spend time with. True, he didn't have a lot of options because the neighborhood was devoid of children during school hours. He was much too social to be a television watcher and he had no cell phone for communication or entertainment. However, I liked thinking that he wouldn't have come had he not enjoyed it to some degree. It's been written that "to be held in the heart of a child is to be a King." I know that for me, it was life-giving to my heart, soul and spirit! I wouldn't trade those day to day bonding years for anything. Never was it an interruption to see him come – only a gladness welling deep in my heart.

I sometimes reflect on the unique bond between grandparents and their grandchildren. For me in my own life, I was fortunate to spend good years with my grandmother – years of my youth. My sister and I looked forward to our summers with her in the small town in which she lived, just ninety miles from our home. We would travel the distance by Greyhound bus. Though only ninety miles, the travel time was three hours because of the mountain roads and countless hairpin curves when speed needed to be reduced to less than thirty-five miles per hour.

Our grandmother would meet us at the bus stop on Main Street; her home was also on Main Street, just a short walk away.

Her house was a large white two-story home with green shutters in the small town of Glenville, WV, which was the County Seat of Gilmer County. It was a sharp contrast to the tiny, one bedroom third-story walk-up apartment that was our home in the city. Every summer, in Glenville, the County Fair would be held at the Fairgrounds just a few miles outside of town. The Fair was primarily 4-H in purpose, but the set-up always included a carousel, a ferris wheel, an array of fine looking animals, cotton candy, arcade games with ball tosses, etc. The Fair was a huge event in the small town of about two thousand people; it was the talk of the town and the county for weeks ahead of time. Most residents wanted to go!

Those days of summer and major holidays were carefree days of playing in our grandmother's large, grassy yard doing cartwheels and handstands with friends, of going barefooted and trying to avoid the many honey bees in the clover of her yards, of Sunday evenings with home churned fresh vanilla or peach ice cream, of sitting on the stairs outside of the parlor, listening to adult conversations of family scandals and town gossip, of reading books by the hours - stories of adventure and escapades. On Saturdays, we were each given a dime so that we could go to the matinee showing of a double-feature movie, usually a Western film. Popcorn was a nickel extra; sometimes we saved our weekly allowance for that. Those were special days which we loved. My grandmother was a widow, and though only in her mid-fifties, she seemed quite old to us with her wire-rimmed glasses, gray hair, cotton house dresses and tie laced shoes. On the other hand, she was spirited with a witty sense of humor and despite the difference in our ages, she was fun to be with. She

Chapter 10

had a vegetable garden that produced tasty fresh food. She had a barn, a cellar, a wash house, a grape arbor, a water well - all manner of things that were different from life in the city. Until I became old enough to get jobs in the summer, I would make the ninety mile bus trip to be with my grandmother almost every summer. I loved her dearly then and always. As the years went by, I began to recognize and value the formative impact upon my life that had been her gift to me and to my sister, Jeanie.

In being fortunate enough to be able to spend quality time with Johnny during his growing-up years, my deep hope is that he, too, will look back upon his days with me with the same savoring of enjoyment that I experienced with my grandmother and that his lifelong love for me will be as strong a love as is possible to have.

CHAPTER 11

MAKE A WISH

*"Faith is the substance of things hoped for,
the evidence of things not yet seen."*
Hebrews 11:1

It was a Thursday evening. Bob and I were reading. Suddenly the front door opened and Johnny came bursting into the living room with news of something that had just happened. Alison was not far behind and the both of them began to tell us why he was so excited.

    Two representatives from The Make A Wish Foundation had come to the Buchanan home to meet with the family. Their purpose was to interview Johnny, to learn about his hopes, his dreams, and his strongest wish as a pre-teen boy. The Make A Wish Foundation is a nationwide, compassionate and generous organization that seeks to grant a "dream wish" for children up to age eighteen, who have life-threatening illnesses that are progressive, degenerative or incurable. A wish experience is frequently a source of inspiration for children undergoing difficult medical treatments and a positive force that helps them overcome their obstacles. Johnny's parents had been contacted by the Foundation to apprise them of his eligibility for this program and to set up an appointment for the interview. Johnny had been thinking about his "dream wish" for quite some time and he was ready to reveal what he hoped would be granted to him. He desired to go on a Disney Cruise to the Caribbean with his family. At that time in his life, he was drawn to water sports, to beaches, to lakes, to swimming pools. He loved to surf, boogie board, fish and do all of the other water activities. He also loved the Disney TV shows and so this combination was dynamite for him. Now it looked as though it could really happen – maybe even this year. He was excited. Between bites of chocolate oreo cookies, he described the interview. His eyes sparkled as he talked about the water slide on the cruise ship that would catapult you into plunging into a deep pool - and of the possibility of riding on the back of a Dolphin as one of the island excursion choices. What fun - what an adventure this would be!!

After Johnny and Alison left, our house was very quiet. Our hearts were silent, too. The ugly side of Cystic Fibrosis had reared its head again - the life-threatening, uncertain head, and the reality of the disease loomed huge in our minds. We were feeling immensely grateful that there is such an organization as the Make A Wish Foundation that seeks to bring joy and happiness to children in seeing a life dream come true. But at the same time, our hearts held a spirit of heaviness that was hard to shake. We were living in the reality of time advancing for Johnny - and still no cure nor major breakthroughs in effective medication treatments. We had hoped to see CF conquered by this time in his life. Promising advancements were on the horizon. We stood on the brink of a potential cure. Time can often be a kind friend. When coupled with hard work, dedicated and skillful researchers who are giving their best to find that cure, I believe that one day we'll see it. In the meantime, we embraced Johnny's world as fully as one could and we entered into his excitement about this cruise with joy, gratitude and high expectations. It's the way that Johnny lives his life - out loud! How could we do less! He has taught us what courage means.

The call came! In December of the year, Johnny and his immediate family had been booked on a Disney Cruise line ship to the Caribbean. It would be a five day trip, requiring a flight to Orlando, FL where the five Buchanans would board the ship. Everything was being arranged and paid for by The Make A Wish Foundation! The Buchanans had only to pack and be ready for the limousine that would pick them up at four a.m. for the trip to the airport. Living just across the street, we, of course, wanted to take pictures of the family getting into the limo. We set our alarm for three-thirty a.m., put on warm jackets, and watched, with cameras poised, from our front porch. However, we hadn't counted on the fact that a black limo would arrive in the darkness of the moonless night, so picture taking would be sketchy at best. We had fun trying, though, and energetically waved them off before going home and tumbling back into bed.

A few months after the trip, Johnny, for a school essay assignment, wrote the following:

JOHNNY'S MEMOIR

"One morning different than any other, my alarm wakes me up at 3:30 a.m. I spring up jumping with joy. I'll tell you why I was very, very happy that morning. At 4:00 a.m., a limo was coming to pick up my family and me to go to LAX. We were flying to Florida to board the "Disney Dream". I'm going to tell you about our time on the cruise ship, and our two ports of call in the Bahamas.

The food on the ship was delicious. The meat was always tender. The first night we were at a "Nemo" themed restaurant. Our waiter, Chris, walked up to us and said, "Hi, we have a very special menu tonight." I thought in my head, "Oh, that's cool!" Then I said, "Chris, can I have some chicken nuggets with BBQ sauce and chocolate milk?" "I hear the chicken nuggets are really good", he said. The second night I had steak and chocolate milk.

Chapter 11

It was so good I had it again the third night. I wish I could have food like that all the time.

When the ship docked, I was so happy because we were in the Bahamas. For the entire day we were at the one and only Atlantis Hotel; that day we got to go swimming with dolphins. We used underwater scooters. It was so cool to feel the water coming off the dolphins' skin. After the dolphins, we went to Atlantis' water park. My brother and I went on a cool slide in an innertube. I felt like it went straight down about 50 feet, then back up a couple of feet. Then we whipped around a corner inside a tube so we wouldn't fly off the edge. The ride ended, along with our day. Atlantis was so fun. I would do it again in a heartbeat!

On Disney's private island, Castaway Cay, we went to a mini recreational center. There was ping pong, basketball, shuffle board, pool, giant chess, and giant checkers. I mainly played basketball. We played a game where whoever made five shots first won. We could play this way because there were three hoops and three balls side by side. Just to let you know, I also beat my brother in shuffleboard.

Our five days on the ship were better than amazing. The thought crossed my mind that maybe one day I could work on a cruise ship. Then I could be on one all the time and get paid for it. After all five days on the ship we will have memories of Atlantis, Castaway Cay, and one full day on the ship. I hope to one day go on a Disney cruise ship again."

Johnny's essay on his dream trip grabbed my heart to the extent that I framed it and hung it on the wall of my office so that I could frequently read it. One day when he was at our house, he took the framed essay to post it in a more prominent place in our home; the wall between the dining room and kitchen was his choice. In that spot it was quite visible for family, friends, guests to see. I loved his boldness in the relocation of it. Today, seven years later, the essay hangs in the dining room of our current home.. My eyes see and read it often and each time, I am heartwarmed by the dream that he had that came true. Now there are different dreams in his heart and he's working hard to make those become a reality. Johnny was then, at eleven years old, an all-in kind of guy. Today he is the same.

Chapter 12

TEAM AWESOME

*"And whatever you do, do it heartily,
as to the Lord and not to men".*
Colossians 3:23

In the spring of the year in Southern California, and all across the nation, in a number of cities and communities, the Cystic Fibrosis Foundation sponsors and organizes 5K walks, called Great Strides Walks. These walks are a major source of fund-raising by the Foundation in continuing to research advancement in the drive to develop breakthroughs and ultimately a cure for Cystic Fibrosis. It was May of the year in 2002 when we learned that Johnny had been diagnosed with CF. The following week, Bob and I were in Escondido, CA visiting with friends for a few days. We saw a flier that was advertising a Great Strides Walk to benefit Cystic Fibrosis. It would take place in Carlsbad, CA – perhaps an hour's drive from Escondido, on the week-end we were to leave for home. We felt the call to battle, so to speak, to actively participate in raising funds that could make a difference in our grandson's life. We quickly wrote letters to friends asking for their support in this Great Strides endeavor. We drove to Carlsbad to join the Great Stride walkers and afterwards headed on home. That was the first of numerous involvements in annual Great Strides walks throughout the years. We would send letters to friends, family, community organizations inviting their participation either in joining the annual walks, donating funds to the Great Strides fund-raising effort – or both. When the Buchanans relocated from Honolulu to the Los Angeles area in 2004, they, too, stepped into a leadership role in promoting the walks.

Every walking family group rallied a team and gave their team a name. When Johnny was a baby, we came up with the name of "Jogging For Johnny". On the day of the walk, balloon bouquets of bright blue and rows of white, canopied tents designated the starting point. T-shirts were given to each walker by The CF Foundation as well as nutrition bars and bottles of water. A program of music, speakers and a continental breakfast launched each walk, which culminated in prizes for dollars raised and a pizza/salad lunch donated by BJ's Restaurant, one of the many sponsors of The Cystic Fibrosis Foundation. The Great Strides Walks provided an important sense of community for the families whose kids were battling this disease on a daily basis. The lively hope of a future cure would be inflamed as families joined together in a common cause. Morale reigned high as perhaps hundreds of walkers, babies in strollers, kids in wagons, dogs of all breeds and sizes strolled, sauntered, or walked briskly along groomed paths or sidewalks in pursuit of making a difference.

Many of the teams designed and purchased their own T-shirts each year to identify their team walkers. One year, Johnny, who was about eleven or twelve at the time, decided that he would like to do the same for his team. Rather than "Jogging for Johnny", he came up with the slogan, "Team Awesome", artistically portrayed in bright yellow letters on a vivid turquoise t-shirt. On the backside of the shirt was a cartoon caricature of a smurf. It seemed that the name of "Jogging For Johnny" was in need of replacement. From Johnny's perspective, I believe it was too tame of a caption to translate the impetus of action and fun that defined his personality. AWESOME connotes "outstanding", "way above the ordinary". The smurf brought humor to the shirt.

Chapter 12

Humor and Johnny are difficult to separate. The shirts were definitely distinctive and a lot of fun to wear. Johnny's leadership skills as well as his tendency to go all-in in making things happen had once again been evidenced. Another year, Bob purchased about fifty small white volleyballs inscribed with "All It Takes Is All You Got". At the time, Johnny was passionately engaged in playing Club Volleyball. On the day of the walk, a number of his friends showed up to walk with the family. Johnny gave each of his team walkers a volleyball as well as anyone else who wanted one. Having the balls for the kids to toss around as they walked kept them from being bored. They also were great keepsakes.

Great Strides events have continued to be the major source of fund-raising that the Cystic Fibrosis Foundation organizes and sets in place each year. People are often drawn to participating in a cause that has grabbed their hearts, for whatever the reason. There is something about putting one foot in front of another, in walking, jogging or running with others united in the same cause, that lifts you to heights of gladness in realizing that you, in conjunction with others, can realistically do something in making a significant difference in lives that need help. Offering your time and energy to a cause greater than your own personal desires rings loud the bell of victory possible. It rallies the heartstrings to not be satisfied with letting others do the work, but to championing a cause yourself.

Chapter 13
FANTASY FUN

"You shall eat in plenty and be satisfied. And praise the name of the Lord your God who has dealt wondrously with you".
Joel 2:26

Most of us in our family are avid movie-goers! Whether in movie theaters or at home on our own television screens, we enjoy the whole experience of watching films. That being said, and also loving celebrations of events, it seemed a natural progression to step into the arena of creating and hosting Oscar parties in our home for our family. And this we did for three years.

We kicked off in 2012 or 2013 with a "Black and White" Oscar event on the Sunday afternoon and evening of the actual Oscar awards that year. Our theme called for everyone to dress in classy black and/or white attire and to bring a black and/or white food item to share. Johnny was excited about this event and on the early afternoon of the party, he came to our house to help. Even as a pre-teen, he still wanted to be a part of whatever was going on. My sister, Jeanie, was visiting with us then and she, Johnny and I were the decorating team that turned our home into a mini Hollywood style Oscar evening fantasyland.

The red carpet entrance into the living room ushered attendees into an elegant scene of black and white balloon bouquets, sparkling gold and silver table fountain sprays, a black tuxedo and red satin gown photo booth, champagne flutes filled with bubbly and a buffet table laden with the most intriguing black and white culinary creations you could imagine. Some that I recall were the adorable black and white penguin

Chapter 13

canapes, black and white deviled eggs, black olives stuffed with cream cheese, oreo cookies, blackened chicken wings, spam musubi, stir-fried steak and white rice. On and on it went. Of course, a golden Oscar trophy was awarded to the person who had top accuracy as to winners in all of the film categories. The evening was incredibly fun, so much so that the unanimous cry went forth – "Let's do it again next year."

And so we did! We decided that our theme would be a Disney one. Each person was to dress as a favorite Disney character and bring food representative of that character or film. Johnny was really into it for this Oscar event. He was the center spoke of the decorating team; Jeanie and I were his assistants. He was filled with ideas and imaginative ways of realizing their development. Through the years Johnny had been a huge Disney fan – of the movies, the TV shows, the characters, so he had both knowledge and heart for this particular theme. On the Saturday prior to Oscar Sunday, he bounded into the house, ready to create his masterpiece, which took a good three or four hours of using a ladder to hang Disney DVD cases from chandeliers and the ceilings as well as artistically taping various Disney posters and pictures on walls and cabinets. The look was "early Disney."

He came back to our home on Sunday to do lettering on large gold foil stars of the names of Oscar nominees and contenders for Best Picture. He rolled out the red carpet that led from the front sidewalk to our front door and living room; then placed and taped down the stars on the carpet to create our own Hollywood Walk of the Stars. Next he hung clumps and bows of red, yellow and black crepe paper streamers around the main part of the house. We added helium balloons in the same colors. The end result was a beautiful Disney Wonderland. Johnny's vision had become reality. Being satisfied with his creation, he raced home to shower and dress. It wasn't long before he returned and when we saw him, Jeanie and I were stunned. He had been transformed into Aladdin; an Aladdin who was strolling on the red carpet like a prince; his outfit of white blouson pants, maroon vest, bare feet, carrying on his head a hemp basket of a long French bread loaf, and a stuffed dangling monkey on his shoulder, was both perfect and captivating. He looked so cool, so suave in his role. How had he done it - working hard on decorations all afternoon, being home for a quick shower and change and then suddenly appearing as a virtual reality Aladdin. Only Johnny!

    Everyone in our family had put energy and time into their character costumes. Several came as swashbuckling pirates, one as Dumbo, another couple as a sorcerer and his broom, another couple as Woody and Jesse from Toy Story. Pocahontas and John appeared as well as a lion and Cinderella, Mickey and Minnie Mouse. Our food dishes were challenging and delicious. The evening was a tremendous success and once again, everyone wanted to do it again the following year.

    By the time the next year had rolled around, we had relocated, moving into our new home in early January. Oscar ceremonies were on the docket for late February and in our minds didn't have a high priority. We were only partially settled, with a great deal of unpacking yet to be done. Not wanting to release the fun of it all and being encouraged by the rest of the family to continue the newly established tradition, we hustled to clear boxes from the main living areas, tucked away the remaining ones and held our third annual Oscar evening - a Pajama Party theme. How easy, and very fun! The food to be brought was to be representative of titles of films or songs in contention

Chapter 13

for the awards. Once again, creativity was flourishing. A most spectacular presentation came in the form of "a bridge of pies", representing the nominated film, Bridge of Spies. Leonardo DiCaprio was up for a Best Actor award that year, and of course, elicited pizzas and antipasta salads. The movie, Moana, was highlighted by teriyaki chicken tenders and sticky rice. Other dishes were equally tied to films of choice.

Johnny didn't feel well that day, but he mustered enough energy to help me anchor down a very long red carpet, made of paper, and quite challenging to work with in the wind that had arisen. He did some lettering of movie titles on gold stars again and then disappeared from sight. Our indoor decorations were skimpy that year - simple posters, stars, and Hollywood signs. Raindrops fell, but didn't dampen our parade. It was dampened though in my heart because Johnny was upstairs in bed while the rest of us were enjoying the evening. Normally when he didn't feel well, he would struggle on, but not on this night. Somehow, the party seemed empty without him. The joy of Johnny was missing!

The third Oscar party brought a conclusion to our Oscar events. Grandkids were becoming engaged and married, some were off to college, other activities were taking precedence. Movies were changing and so were we. For three consecutive years, we had been captured by celebrating together as a family the glitter and glamor of the film industry. Fun times had reigned and memories would linger for a lifetime. Hooray for Hollywood!

Chapter 14
THE POWER OF TRADITION

"The Lord has done great things for us and we are glad!"
Psalm 126:3

For over fifty years now, the Buchanan clan have gathered for annual reunion days near Searchlight, NV at a site on Lake Mohave called Cottonwood Cove. Johnny's great grandpa Brown, his children and their families were the core group that launched this remarkable tradition. When they first began to converge, it was in tents in a primitive setting with very limited facilities. Rattlesnakes were at times spotted in the area. As the Brown kids grew up and married, the tradition of a summer week together at the lake continued – and grew larger in number. Some years later, a businessman built a twenty-four room motel on the property and established a marina. For years, in late July or early August, the Buchanans, Smiths, Browns and other siblings and families of the original Brown family, have rented most of, if not the entire motel, for five to seven days. Those who have boats bring them and share with those who don't. In the early morning hours, at the breaking of dawn, the lake is as smooth as glass, perfect for water-skiing, tubing, jet-skiing, etc. Young and old alike arise in the dark to quickly dress and gravitate to their boats docked just yards away at the marina. Boat owners and their kids are eager to get out on the water for several hours of fun before the waters are roughened by the wind, the sun and other boaters.

Bob and I had joined the families for several years, bringing some of our other grandchildren with us. We were able to experience the magnetism of that which has drawn the families to return to the shores of the lake year after year. It has nothing to do with the accommodations nor the food, nor the ease of making it all happen, for each of those presents its difficulties. It has everything to do with time-honored family traditions, family relationships and rare boating and water sports fun with family. The motel itself is a simple structure, a low-lying, single-story building, built in a horseshoe fashion with all of the rooms facing the lake. A lawn in front of the motel provides a great play area for small children as well as a gathering spot for large groups eating together in the evenings. Bar-b-q grills are spaced intermittently throughout the curvature of the lawn area, making it easy to both cook and share food with your neighbor.

The curvature of the Cove is such that it forms a natural beach area with ample sand and the safety that allows for relaxed swimming and cooling off from the daytime temperatures that will often rise to over 115 degrees. The cove is ideal for small children; for anyone who wants to enjoy refreshing water play. The Cove beach itself is roped off from the rest of the lake. Families bring beach and sand chairs, umbrellas, shade awnings and canopies, balls and sand toys of all kinds and vitally important, a generous supply of sunscreen as protection against the sweltering summer sun of the desert area. When it's just too uncomfortable outdoors, people tend to retreat to their air-conditioned rooms of the motel to relax, play games for hours, nap or have conversations. Cooking is kept to a minimum with much of the food having been prepared at home and transported in gigantic ice chests. The closest town for purchasing supplies is Searchlight, eleven miles away, so trips to "the store" are kept to a minimum, if at all. The Marina houses a tiny shop, primarily stocking souvenirs, basic swim gear, emergency supplies, soft drinks, popsicles and ice creams of various kinds. The store management provides one complimentary small bag of cocktail ice per day to the motel guests; other, larger bags may be purchased. Each motel room has a tiny, dorm-sized refrigerator, which is helpful, and of course, a bathroom sink for cleaning up dishes. Paper products are much more popular to use and toss.

Other than boating and water play, one of the highlight attractions for the kids, teens and younger adults has to do with the large rock cliffs that flank one side of the lake. The cliffs range in size from a height of perhaps ten or twelve feet above the water when it is low, to over fifty feet or so. Jumping off of a cliff into the water is a hallmark moment each year as every jumper attempts to beat their record height jump of the previous year, generally aspiring to the next level when he or she returns to the Cove again. Even if you've reached the pinnacle, you're ready to do it again next time because it's enthusiastically described as a blast of fun.

All of these activities, competitions, games, water sports, conversations have been a strong force in cementing relationships with cousins, aunts, uncles and grandparents that continue through the years to not only sustain, but grow. It's often difficult to get together during the course of the year, but Mohave is indeed a high priority that is honored year after year. It's an amazing thing to see the depth of the desire in the hearts of the Buchanan Clan to set aside time each year, regardless of whatever other opportunities or events clamor for attention, to ensure that they will be a part of the Mohave vacation with all of the greater family. Johnny talks a lot about Mohave days and the outlandishly fun times that he has each year. He would never want to miss it. In fact, in recent years, he and others in his family have joined with his dad's brothers and their families to do some tent camping and boating at Mohave in September or October of the year during Public Schools Fall break of about four days.

This mini-vacation is becoming a uniquely special time, too!

In this day and age of high tech involvements, fractured relationships, social pressures, disintegration of family values, national disharmony and self-centered achievement at all costs, it's a beautiful thing to see a large clan of sixty to one hundred or so release attachment to their cell phones (minimal service at Cottonwood Cove) and the comforts of home in order to dig in and work hard to help make Mohave continue to take place in the hearts and lives of the aged as well as the new, young generations coming up the pike, those on the road to building their families and the valued traditions and the memories that will prove to be impacting and influential in their lives. 2020 saw the celebration of fifty years of Mohave days. That in and of itself was a most remarkable achievement to applaud.

CHAPTER 15

A NEW DIRECTION

"Behold, I will do a new thing. Now it shall spring forth."
Isaiah 43:18

Johnny's Jr. High days had come to an end. He had been a vibrant part of the life of Trinity Classical Academy with fine achievements in academics, athletics and leadership. His winsome, witty personality had been embraced by faculty and peers alike. His spirit seemed indomitable as he pressed on in spite of ups and downs with his health which would necessitate his being absent from classes. He worked hard to keep on top of things, having an inner drive to give of his best.

Now it was time to move on into high school at Trinity. Trinity is a Christian Classical School of the highest caliber, providing excellent, stimulating education that well prepares students to be qualified to enter almost any college or university in our nation. The standards are high; the demands of time spent on homework are equally high. Absenteeism at the high school level can be a cruel tyrant in putting you in arrears with your studies. As his freshman year unfolded, there began to be concerns in Johnny's mind regarding the necessary tune-up hospitalizations, class time missed and the sacrifices that would be required to keep achieving at Trinity. He also had a growing desire for more volleyball in his life. Trinity had no high school boys volleyball team. Johnny had lobbied to see one launched, but it had become apparent that the time wasn't right for that formation yet. The seeds of transferring to another high school were growing in his mind and taking root.

Chapter 15

It had been during Johnny's junior high years and his freshman high school year that he had become involved in helping Alison at times when she would be coaching girls volleyball teams at Trinity. Later on she coached girls teams at Legacy Volleyball Club in Santa Clarita and he stepped into helping there as well. He loved being on the volleyball court, shagging balls, helping with set-ups and clean-ups and in general, just being available for whatever was needed. During the course of all of this, his natural talent for the game began to be strengthened. He realized that though he was a fine athlete in most sports he'd been involved in, volleyball was his passion - a sport that drove him to "try and catch excellence." Eventually he was spending hours on the volleyball courts, practicing, practicing, practicing. Almost any time the gym courts were open, Johnny would be there, helping any coach who needed him. In large letters on a wall of the Legacy Club gym, there is a slogan which reads, "It's not the will to win...it's the will to prepare to win..." Johnny's desire to transfer into a public high school that had a strong volleyball program became of prime importance in his mind. Though he was playing on a Legacy Club team by this time, his heart was crying out for more and more volleyball. He began to research the public high schools in the Santa Clarita Valley. He lived in the district to attend Saugus High School, but Saugus wasn't as strong in volleyball as West Ranch High or Valencia High. West Ranch offered not only a top volleyball program but a split school schedule which Johnny was used to at Trinity and liked. He and his parents had conversations regarding his transfer desire. Alison and Mike prayed about it and ultimately, believing this plan would be best for Johnny, set up interviews with the Saugus principal. God opened the door for releasing him as a Saugus student and opened wide the door into acceptance by West Ranch. We were all elated - Johnny's joy could hardly be contained. But then why should it have to be!

He entered West Ranch High in August of 2017 as a sophomore. He knew only a handful of students in a population group of about 2,500 or so. That wasn't a problem. He had a confidence in being where he was supposed to be and an attitude of making a difference. While in the process of requesting the transfer, and prior to his admittance, Johnny had submitted his application for the ASB leadership class. An interview with an administrative faculty member was required. The end result was: "Thank you for stepping up to apply. We would encourage you to do so again next semester after you've been on campus long enough to become acquainted with the school. It's apparent that you have leadership qualities." Johnny did re-apply for the second semester; he was accepted and served with dedication and enthusiasm during the entirety of his high school years.

West Ranch High was a perfect fit for him. He thrived as an active part of the student body life of the school, showing up for spirit rallies, football and basketball games, proms and dances. Academically, his grades were above average, and socially, he became involved with a group of friends who were leaders on campus. His character, keenness of mind, humor, hard work and spirit of help were magnetic attractions to both teachers and students. My word descriptions of Johnny fall far short of the aura of Johnny that draws people to him in recognition of the uniqueness of this young man. He's fascinating as he tells stories of the happenings of his days. I find myself, time and again, intrigued by this grandson of mine. He is a true "force of nature", unstoppable, dynamic, yet tenderly compassionate. John Michael Kupono Buchanan has already made his mark upon the world in which he lives!

CHAPTER 16
BENCHMARK MOMENTS

*"Wait on the Lord. Be of good courage,
and He shall strengthen your heart."*
Psalm 27:14

Johnny's dream of playing high school volleyball was turning into reality. He was one of only two sophomores who made the Varsity Team at West Ranch High. He was slated to be a setter. A setter in volleyball is comparable to the role of quarterback on a football team. Both positions are considered to be the brains behind the game. Both require keen athletic IQ's, quick hands, a mind that can swiftly assess the moment and make adjustments, accuracy in placing the ball, and high energy. It was an ideal position for Johnny. However, the West Ranch volleyball team already had an outstanding setter, Tyson - a senior; he would be playing full games throughout the season.

Looking upon his varsity placement as being an opportunity, partially, to observe and study Tyson, Johnny concentrated on doing so in order to sharpen and improve his own skills. Naturally, he wanted as much play as possible; he hoped that the coach would give him chances to be in the game. He was willing to bide his time, and wait for his turn as primary setter. In the meantime, he drilled on refining his entire game as well as his jump serving skills. Initially that proved to be his entry point into getting into the games; the coach would put Johnny in when it was vitally important to land a good serve. Johnny produced and the coach gave him increasingly more chances to do so. The season moved on and Johnny with it. He had shown himself to be a valuable contributor to the success of the team. On the court, his energy dominated and revved up the other players. Frequently he was the spark that was needed to bring the victories.

His sophomore year brought not only a good start to his Varsity Volleyball life, but to high school life in general. He had a number of good friends that he hung out with - Kylie, Aidan, Maggie, Drew, Neiko, Zack, Jadyn, Maya, Dom, Isa and Allison to name a few. Johnny's health remained fairly stable to the extent that he was able to be fully engaged in classes, activities, volleyball, social events and other interests that drew his attention and time. Life was good, with the promise of it continuing to be so. The transfer into West Ranch High School seemed to have provided all that Johnny had envisioned.

In April of his sophomore year, he had to enter Children's Hospital, LA (CHLA) for a "power boost". He was in the hospital for two weeks, and when released, he felt great. But several weeks later, in May, we were stunned when he had to be airlifted by helicopter to CHLA because of severe chest pains – something he'd never experienced before. What was going on? This time in the hospital, he was under Cardiac care. Family and friends flocked to the hospital with balloons, games, gifts, sweets and hours of visiting. Families and friends from around the nation – and some internationally, were praying for Johnny. I remember times when I would be driving, with tears flooding my eyes, rolling down my face, shouting and imploring God to save our Johnny - to take me, instead, that he might live. Nothing substantiates that God works in that way but I was desperate in my prayers. Initial tests indicated myocarditis or a thickening of a portion of the lining of the wall of his heart. Appropriate treatment was initiated. However, further tests were not conclusive. After two weeks of hospitalization and diagnostic

Chapter 16

testing, perplexed specialists had no definitive diagnosis other than a probable myocarditis. What caused it wasn't known; what would resolve it would be rest. Upon discharge, Johnny and his parents were told that he should restrict any physical activity for a period of three to six months in order to give his heart adequate time to heal. A follow-up check by his local pediatrician some days later resulted in a clean bill of health, with no physical limitations required. The differing opinions were a puzzlement!

Ten days after discharge, he played in a weekend Club volleyball tournament, running hard, diving for balls with uncurbed energy. Six weeks later, he traveled to Phoenix, AZ with his Club team and played four days of volleyball competition in the USA Jr. Nationals Boys Volleyball Tournament. Out of the hundreds of teams that played, his team won the Gold Medal that year. It is many years later now; he is still vigorously competing and his heart remains healthy.

In allowing Johnny to return to volleyball play much sooner than had been advised by hospital physicians, Alison and Mike were following the pattern of their beliefs; the belief of letting Johnny live his life to the fullest for as long as God had for him. Johnny had proven himself to be mature, with sound judgment; they trusted him to assess well, to think in long-range terms and to not take foolish risks. They prayed for God's guidance and wisdom to be made known to them concerning matters of their children.

Some will ask, what happened in May of that year in regard to Johnny's heart? Was it an uncertain diagnosis or a true miracle of healing! We chose to believe that God had granted the favor of wellness for Johnny at that time and simply moved across the medical cautions and recommendations with fullness of life for him. In our family, we call that a miracle!

The summer months brought not only the fun and success of volleyball play but a significant change in the family life of the Buchanans. Deja, the eight year old beautiful black labrador pet, began to decline in health. Deja was the daughter of Shadow, the first dog pet the kids had ever had. Shadow, at age thirteen, was content to rest and keep a watchful eye on the family. Deja was energetic and playful. When it became obvious that she was failing in her ability to walk or stand, the family vet's exam revealed a tumor, most likely cancerous, that wasn't really operable. He recommended, in all kindness to Deja, that she be put to sleep. Johnny was part of the team of family kids who carried Deja to the car and bravely accompanied her to the vet's office for their final act of love to her. It was painful to watch. The next day Johnny took the pink collar that Deja had worn around her neck for years and placed it on the wooden cross that stood visibly tall in his backyard. It was the same cross that he had fashioned about six years earlier. The cross and the collar are still there, both weathered by the years but ever a heartful reminder of the loyalty of a pet who gave her "all" in love to her family, and of a Savior who gave His "all" in love to redeem a lost world. Such is the hallmark of love!

Almost seven months later, in the spring of the year, we lost Shadow, too, to cancer. Once again, the kids carried a beloved pet to the car for the trip to the vet's office. Shadow had always worn a purple collar; Johnny hung her collar on the backyard cross right alongside of Deja's pink one. Looking out from our family room window, our foreground view is of the cross with the two collars hanging on it in criss/cross fashion. The family pets were gone, but never the memories nor the love!

Johnny & Alison

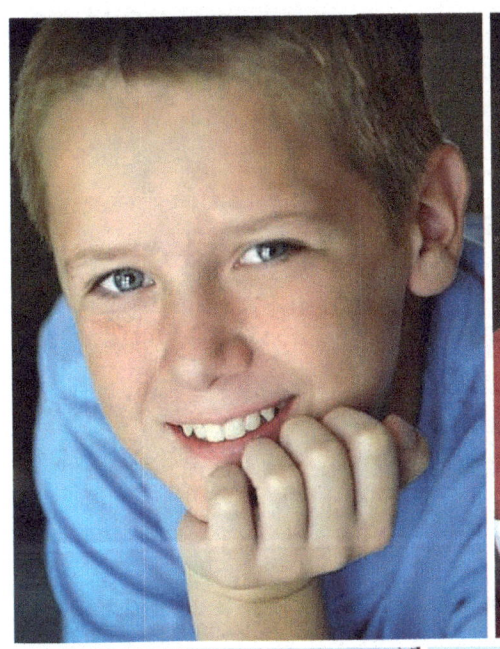

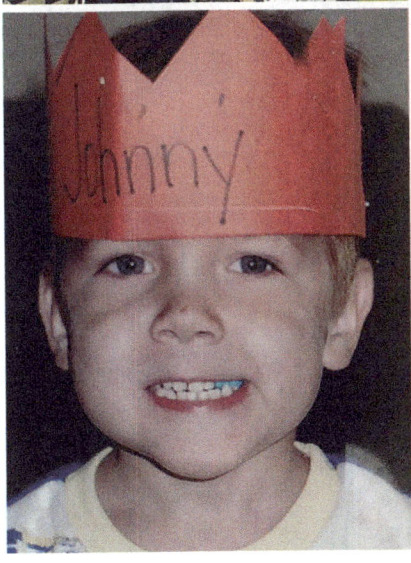

L-R: Emily, Johnny, Chris, Alison & Mike Buchanan at the 2016 Summer Olympics in Rio de Janeiro

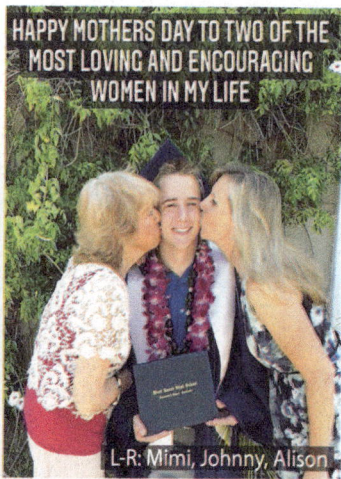

HAPPY MOTHERS DAY TO TWO OF THE MOST LOVING AND ENCOURAGING WOMEN IN MY LIFE

L-R: Mimi, Johnny, Alison

Linda & Keith Buchanan (Grandparents)

Mimi Emy (Author) & Papa Bob Augur (Grandparents)

2005 Family Cruise

Johnny

Johnny & Kiba

Sports

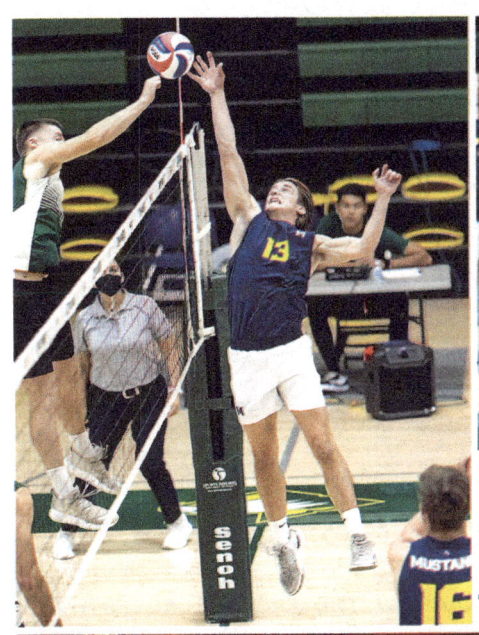

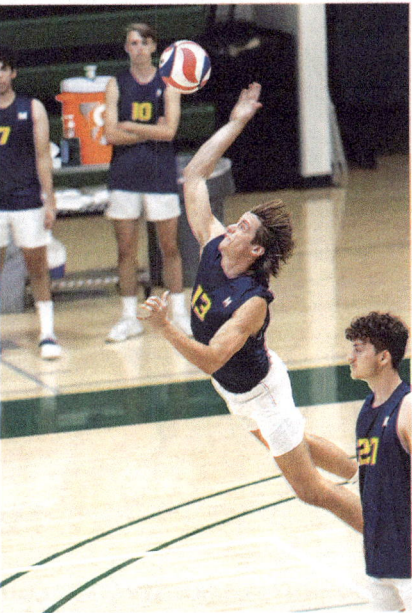

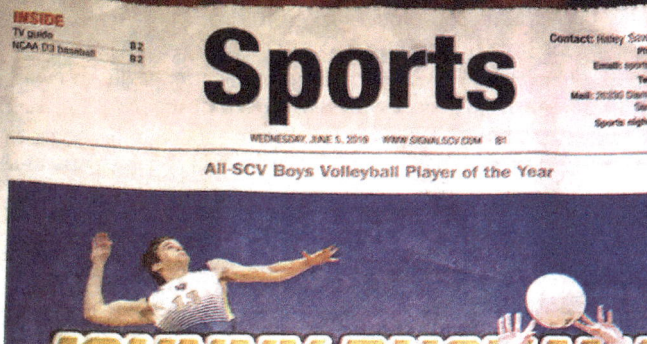

All-SCV Boys Volleyball Player of the Year

Setting for success

Boys volleyball: West Ranch's Johnny Buchanan led Foothill League in assists, his team in aces

calhope_courage An April recipient of the CalHOPE Courage Award, Johnny Buchanan, a freshman on The...

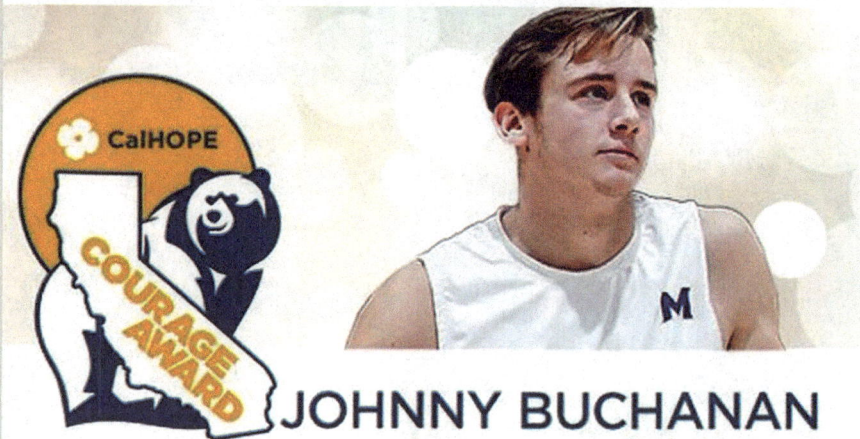

JOHNNY BUCHANAN
The Master's University | *Volleyball*

JOHNNY DEMONSTRATED COURAGE IN THE FACE OF ADVERSITY battling Cystic Fibrosis his whole life, preventing him from developing his mind and his body. Being immunocompromised put his dream of playing college volleyball on hold during COVID-19. After transferring from a community college to The Master's University, he excelled academically and was a key contributor to the Mustangs' successful season. A Kinesiology & P.E. major he relies upon his Faith to balance living with CF with achieving his goals.

> "He who overcomes, I will make him a <u>pillar</u> in the sanctuary of My God, and he will never go out from it anymore. And I will write on him the name of My God and the name of the city of My God, the new Jerusalem, which comes down out of heaven from My God, and My new name."
> Revelation 3:12

This drawing by Johnny while serving as a Christian camp counselor in 2022, conveys his passionate desire to build his life upon the strong foundation of the God whom he loves & serves.

Part II - The Transformational Years

Chapter 17
UNSTOPPABLE QUEST

*"Do you see a man who excels in his work;
he will stand before kings."*
Proverbs 22:29 (NKJV)

Suddenly, or so it seemed, it was mid-August of 2018. The summer had been filled with variety and adventure for Johnny - adventures both anticipated and unexpected. A week at Hume Lake Christian Camp with high school friends, the week with his family at Mohave Lake, the USA Boys Junior Nationals Volleyball Tournament in Phoenix, AZ where the Legacy Club sixteen year-old boys team competed hard, ending up with Johnny's team capturing the Gold Medal honors; these were indeed highlight experiences. The game was a thrilling conclusion to the four day competition event: live-streamed broadcasted play on Center Court of the Convention Center which had grandstand seating. A full house of spectators watched. The atmosphere was electric. The Legacy Club winners were garlanded with gold medal ribbons and presented with a handsome championship trophy. Spirits reigned high as the boys left the Convention Center accolades to join families and friends for some raucous celebrating before heading home to Los Angeles. Alison, Mike, Bob and I had watched every game of the four day tournament. We were so proud and happy for Johnny and the Legacy Club team. Those moments of dauntless effort and final victory are yet alive to me.

Johnny had been invited to participate in a USA High Performance Developmental Volleyball Camp in the Chicago, Illinois area; another four days of non-stop volleyball were to be his. There were major expense commitments involved in making the trip but the possible became a reality and Johnny and his parents boarded the red-eye flight with keen anticipation of the unique experience that lay before them.

The participating teams at the camp were made up of sixteen year-old boys from across the nation - boys who had qualified by their performance in try-outs earlier in the year. Johnny knew no one who would be attending this camp, but he was excited to get to play with, who he hoped would be, highly competitive and skilled players who would challenge him. He was striving to keep advancing in mastering the game, both as a setter and as an all-around top player. He desired to play with guys who were seeking to play collegiate ball or perhaps even Olympic ball. Those were Johnny's goals and he was consumed in working hard to obtain them. In the end, he felt that the camp immersion had been a valuable one, beneficial to both his game and his volleyball resume, so to speak. His parents had taken advantage of a few of the days when teams were just practicing to engage in some sight-seeing in the Chicago area. The three returned home, grateful for the respective awakenings each had experienced. Johnny was having the time of his life, as well as accumulating medals and awards. He was on what I called "his Olympic Victory March." It seemed as though the accelerated physical activity level of the entire summer belied the cautionary medical recommendations that Johnny had received in May, just a few short months prior, recommendations for a summer of rest and cessation of physical activity. He had no time for, nor interest in that!

Chapter 17

Mixed in with all of the organizational activities of the summer were days of hanging out with friends, hikes in the neighborhood hills, day trips to the beach, family get-togethers and celebrations; on and on it went. Once in a while, a lazy, laid-back day would occur; more often late nights and early mornings were the norm. It was Johnny's first summer of stepping into that long-awaited world of the freedom of driving and he was loving every minute of it. In a way, it represented a "rite of passage". He had the use of a family car, a pale, yellow 2003 Volkswagen, black topped convertible. What a cool car for a teen-ager to drive, especially in California when generally, year round, the top could be down; the wind-tousled look of the longish hair of Johnny was a magnet for the girls. Johnny was tall and handsome, like a Madison Avenue fashion model. He had warned us that once he was a licensed driver, we wouldn't see much of him. This was proving to be the case. He had parental permission to go where he did; he was usually respectful of the curfews and responsible about checking in upon arriving home in the evenings. Who could ask for more from a teen-aged son. He was a sixteen year old boy with dreams in his heart, making them happen! These days were not to be taken for granted, for like a silent enemy lying in wait, Cystic Fibrosis was ever an underlying threat which continued to claim the lives of too many young people around the world. A cure hadn't been discovered yet. But thankfully, the status of the disease had gone from incurable to life-threatening. That was indeed a measure of progress.

Shortly after classes were underway in his junior year, Johnny had been contacted by a student in the Communications ASB leadership class at West Ranch High to ask if he would be willing to do an interview having to do with "how as an outstanding athlete, he had learned to overcome adversity and embrace the challenges in his life to keep a positive mindset." The interview would be videoed and shown at one of the weekly general assemblies at the school, most likely in late September or October. Johnny agreed to do the interview. This was a huge step for him. He had never tried to withhold the fact that he had an incurable disease, but neither had he chosen to broadcast it. As an incoming tenth grader, in a health class, for a written and oral assignment, he had chosen the topic of Cystic Fibrosis. I'm not sure if at that time, he "owned" CF, or if it was simply a factual, generalized information paper. Most of the student body, except for close friends, probably had very little idea of what CF was, nor how Johnny dealt with it on a daily basis. In fact, just the opposite. The disease that he was born with belied the way in which he was living his life. His full energy and stamina gave no hint of the condition that he brought into every facet of his life.

The September interview was remarkable. Johnny articulated so well, with clarity and transparency, in explaining the genetic cause of CF, the practical application of daily treatments, what it was like to live with CF and how he chose to cope with it. I had never been more proud of him in all of his life. This is a stellar statement because I've always been his champion, so very proud of him for who he is as a person, for who he is in every arena of his life; his intellect, his exuberant joy, his optimistic outlook. Without any shadow of turning, he has been MY HERO from the time that he was a young lad and my eyes and ears were opened to the non-complaining, consistently positive, overcoming way in which he was choosing to move on in life. Though encumbered by hours of tedious treatments each day, his innate joy was bubbling over in an infectiously captivating manner. One could almost forget that at the time of his youth, CF was considered to be a fatal disease. He was too young then to fully understand CF, but he was old enough to

Chapter 17

be observing that his brother and sister didn't have to undergo all of the daily treatment regimen that he did. He must have wondered why! But now he was a high school student and he knew CF well.

When I watched his interview on YouTube, my pride in him swelled to such a level that I thought my heart would burst wide open, again and again. Tears of awe, tears of joy, tears of thankfulness all mingled together in running down my face. As well as I knew him, I was still amazed at his poise, his wordage, his openness and veracity of explanation of life with CF before an entire student body. In his clear, concise manner, he was giving his peers an insight into his life on a daily basis, not only as an athlete, but as a teen-ager. After watching the interview, I sought him out, hugged him ever so tightly and told him that in a whole lifetime of being over the top proud of him, I had never been more so than in watching the interview. I was humbled in thinking that God had allowed us the privilege of having such a young man in our family. I'm now including some quotes from Johnny's interview.

"This is my fifth year now of playing volleyball. I started playing because I wanted to go to the practices when my mom was coaching my sister's team, and it was a lot of fun. I loved it from the time I first started playing it. The owner of the Club asked me to play for him, and I did. When I'm on the court, I try to block from my mind everything else from outside of the court. I just love to play the game. I love it a lot and that's why I'm still playing it. It's a good feeling. The biggest problem that I face on the court is cardio, which was the same for basketball or any other sport that I've played because Cystic Fibrosis affects your lungs. Cystic Fibrosis is a genetic, chronic disease which means that you were born with it and you'll have it your whole life span.

It affects your lungs by producing a thicker, stickier mucous than most people have. CF affects my life a lot on a day to day basis. I have to take a good amount of pills and treatments and use a nebulizer every day. I have a vest that I wear in the morning and evening for thirty minutes at a time that helps in physically shaking out the mucous , along with saline solutions which help in thinning out the mucous in order to cough it up. With fitting in all of my treatments as well as school, homework and volleyball, I don't have much down time. Here at school, I try and stay positive and active with volleyball and whatever else I'm involved in. To other people who have Cystic Fibrosis I would say, stay as active as possible. Any doctor will tell you how important that is. Try and stay on top of your treatments in order to stay out of the hospital. Don't let CF weigh you down, but try and embrace it, and if you can, use it for a positive thing in your life."

Johnny's junior year at West Ranch was characterized by the same drive and passion that he had shown as a sophomore student. Up at six a.m. to be out the door and on time for his seven a.m. classes. ASB involvement was huge; he devoted countless hours to making posters and banners for organized sports, games and rallies, to decorating the gym for these events, school dances, proms, etc. Varsity volleyball as well as Club volleyball practices and week-end tournaments brought opportunities for him to engage in that which he loved most of all - playing volleyball at a highly competitive level: learning, developing, improving not only his serving and setting skills, but ratcheting up his game as an all-around player. Injuries began to plague his season; he pressed on, rarely giving way to not being on the court. He appeared to handle the various injuries with wise care and sheer determination to not give in. He refused to be stopped.

Chapter 17

During his pre-school and elementary school years, he had not been one to sit and watch television. However he was drawn to movies having to do with those who rose above the obstacles and circumstantial limitations of their lives to display a positivity of outlook and an attitude of finding a way to persevere and have fun with it all. Movies such as The Blind Side, Soul Surfer, and Spirit were his early age companions. I recall that the song from the movie, Spirit, that he loved to listen to over and over again had the lyrics of , "Get off of my back and out of my head - I wanna be free." As a youngster, one with a strong will, he had fiercely set a course from which he never veered - a "force of nature" course, a force to be reckoned with! It was the kind of stuff that makes heroes of men and women!

Christmas of 2018 was approaching and four of the five Buchanans were packing to fly to Italy to join with Emily who was in the Pepperdine University Sophomore European Study Abroad program for the academic year. Christopher, who had been seeing a bit of Germany, united with Alison and Mike in Rome. Johnny, because of final exam schedules, flew by himself to Rome to join his family. Being together for Christmas, staying in an Air B&B near St. Peter's Square and The Vatican, was an experience of a lifetime. Their Christmas tree was a tiny one that had been spotted in the trash nearby and hand carried to their small apartment room. Alison decorated it with a few Christmas cards and little gifts that were tucked in suitcases. The weather was cold and damp; a few days before leaving Italy, Johnny became ill with a bad cold. From a sick bed, his impression of Italy wasn't a favorable one. It brightened up considerably, at least momentarily, when his family found a Subway Sandwich Shop and brought Johnny's favorite sub sandwich to him. As I recall the story, he ate it with "happiness tears" running down his face. Perhaps Italy had something to be said for it after all. But in reality, even after travelling to see the sights of Florence, the Amalfi Coast and Venice over the course of the two week vacation, Johnny's thoughts concerning the appeal of Italy could be simply stated in that "he had seen enough of the nation to last quite a while." He was ecstatic to be returning home in early January.

Chapter 18
A FORCE OF NATURE

"The Lord is with you, you mighty man of valor."
Judges 6:12

How do you define "a force of nature? Webster's dictionary defines it as "strength or energy of an exceptional degree, an influence that causes motion or a change of motion, to raise or accelerate to the utmost." I define it as my grandson, Johnny! I base this not entirely on my own observations and interactions with him, but on an internationally accepted assessment that reveals personal strengths and talents. Alison is working in an organization by the name of CoreClarity, which actually, through a twenty minute assessment and diagnostic evaluation, hallmarks an individual's top five strengths. That information gives a clear picture of a particular category in which the person falls. Johnny, at age sixteen, was assessed as "a force of nature". None of us in the family were at all surprised by this. From childhood days to teen years, he had blazed a trail of making things happen. Unchartered waters were a magnet to him. It was fascinating to watch the unbelievable way in which he pioneered both cause and effect, rather like being a thermostat instead of a thermometer. A thermometer registers what is; a thermostat causes change.

As he stepped into 2019, he continued to be focused on life as an athlete - as a rising volleyball star, on life as a leader in high school, life as a dedicated student. High school volleyball dominated his days. Friends were vitally important to him; kids liked being around him. He was engaged in gym workouts, hiking with friends, tryouts for USA Junior Boys National summer teams/camps and a whole host of other activities. Motion seemed to be a source of his thriving.

May was approaching and commensurately the annual end-of-school year events; the junior/senior prom, yearbook distribution, sports banquets, trips to Disneyland, final exams and other activities. The Volleyball Sports Banquet was a huge target highlight for Johnny. The catered event was held at the lovely Valencia Country Club. Parents and families dressed up for the occasion, as did the athletes. Johnny received noteworthy awards.

On Saturday, May 18, 2019, the front page of the Sports Section of THE SIGNAL, the local Santa Clarita Valley newspaper, ran headlines of "WILDCATS SETTER WINS PLAYER OF THE YEAR". The caption read: BOYS VOLLEYBALL; BUCHANAN STEPPED INTO THE STARTING SETTER ROLE AND FLOURISHED. The article went on to say, "West Ranch boys volleyball starting setter, Junior Johnny Buchanan had only played a total of 31 games at the varsity level. Buchanan never backed down from the challenges, excelling and being named the Foothill League Player of the Year. "It was really cool just knowing that I would have that position and have the opportunity to lead my team to another Foothill League championship", Buchanan said of his role at the beginning of the season. "It was always my goal from the beginning of the season, but I never really thought about it during league play because we were just focused on winning as a team. It just became a by-product of wanting that league championship".

"The chemistry with his teammates was noticeable from the start as he stepped into the starting setter position

Chapter 18

and delivered 26 assists in the first match of the season in a 3-1 win over Simi Valley. With every game that West Ranch played, it seemed like Buchanan's dynamic athleticism flourished more and more as he grew closer with his teammates.

Ranking top five on the team in almost every statistical category, Buchanan did a little bit of everything for West Ranch's fourth straight undefeated Foothill League title season. He ended his junior year as the team leader with 839 assists and 56 aces, second with 51 total blocks (27 solo), third with 135 digs and occasionally made a kill here and there to finish fifth on the team with 86 kills."

"Just focusing at every practice, taking every rep seriously and getting better," Buchanan said. "Playing for all my teammates every game and trying to make them look as good as possible. I just want to give a shout out to all my teammates, Zach Drake, Neiko Pittman, and Spencer Birchal," Buchanan said. "I couldn't have done it without them. It's a team game, it's never just one person's responsibility for any win or loss throughout the season."

On Wednesday, June 5, 2019, Johnny again made the front page of The Signal's Sports section with a couple of pictures and the captions: SETTING FOR SUCCESS; "West Ranch's Johnny Buchanan earned the starting setter position this season and excelled, leading to his ALL-SANTA CLARITA VALLEY BOYS VOLLEYBALL PLAYER OF THE YEAR AWARD." This was quite amazing! As a junior with only one season behind him of being a setter, Johnny had captured both the Foothill League Player of the Year award for boys volleyball and the All-Santa Clarita Valley Boys Volleyball Player of the Year award!" Once again, this proud grandma ran to the grocery stores to buy nine copies of the newspaper to send to relatives back east. I had done this in May as well, so I knew just where the newsracks were located.

The June 5th featured article read: "Playing sparingly in his sophomore and first year of playing varsity boys volleyball for West Ranch, setter Johnny Buchanan patiently waited behind senior setter Tyson Drake for his time to shine as the starting setter. Growing up watching Tyson and playing alongside his brother Zack Drake at Legacy Volleyball Club, Johnny was able to observe what it took to be a leader on the court and through hard work, passion and dedication, Buchanan was named the starting setter and a season later, win the All-SCV Boys Volleyball Player of the Year Award".

"I knew I had to fill Tyson's shoes and they were big shoes to fill since he had been starting for the past couple of years on varsity", Buchanan said. "I've known Tyson and looked up to him since I was in 7th grade. Getting to fill his shoes was kind of a big opportunity for me". Shouldering the responsibility of being the team's starting setter in his junior year, Buchanan excelled in almost every statistical category. His precision hitting led him to finish with 86 kills. His biggest contribution to the team came at his natural position, setter, as he paced the team and finished the season as the Foothill League leader in assists with 839 on the year.

"The goal was to win league again and go further in playoffs than we did last year", Buchanan said, "which we obviously accomplished this year and we did much more. Putting in that work every practice and keeping the focus on the goals kind of made the All-SCV Player of the Year award happen on it's own. It was always my goal to help the team do better and so I did what I could to accomplish the goals for the team and this just came along with that".

Putting his own ambitions and well-being behind the

betterment of the team and ultimate goal, Buchanan battled injuries throughout the year. He dealt with knee problems during the regular season, a dislocated thumb in the regular season finale against Valencia and a bruised shoulder in playoffs that made it almost impossible to not feel the pain every time he hit the ball. Pushing through it all, Buchanan and the Wildcats won their fourth straight undefeated Foothill League title and earned a top seed in the CIF-Southern Section Division 2 playoffs. Ultimately the team fell in the 3rd round of play to the eventual Division 2 Champions, Saddleback Valley Christian.

Buchanan has a pretty busy summer filled with tremendous volleyball opportunities before returning for his senior season at West Ranch. He will join Legacy Volleyball Club and compete in the Junior Olympics in Dallas, TX in the first week of July before heading east to South Carolina for USA Volleyball A2 Camp for the last week of July. "I'm hoping to come out with another medal because we won gold last year in our division", Buchanan said of the performance in the 2018 Junior Olympics.

And indeed, when the dust was settled in Dallas at the end of the Fourth of July week, the Legacy Volleyball Club was victorious, having garnered the Silver Medal honors. Tough competition between hundreds of teams vying for win after win had ultimately resulted in Legacy playing on Center Court in the Gold Medal match. The game was hard fought; Johnny had pressed on relentlessly for four days of vigorous play, refusing to give in to a hurting ankle. Once again, the talented, hard-driving setter had led his team to Center Court for the final game of the 2019 Olympics for seventeen year old boys. The Gold was within reach, but in the end, it was the Silver that the boys took home. This was the third consecutive year that Johnny's team had taken either Gold or Silver honors. How proud we were of their distinguished awards and the way in which the boys had competed. How grateful we, as a family were, for the opportunity that Johnny had to play on a strongly competitive, high-caliber team - with his dedicated mind-set, his outstanding skills and his health all working together for top performance and fun!

Dallas itself was a jewel of a place to spend four or five days. Alison, Mike, Bob and I were glued to the Convention Center in watching the games of course, but there were breaks and free times available to do some city sight-seeing and to seek out and dine on the famous Texas-style bar-b-que meats and specialties. The team boys and some in their families had fun riding the electric scooters around the town. Bob and I participated vicariously, wishing we were balanced enough to actually ride them. We had to be content with maneuvering around via Uber; that was great fun for us. We actually felt pretty trendy in doing so.

On to South Carolina for the A2 Developmental Camp and another opportunity for Johnny to play with sharp volleyball players from other parts of the nation. Mike was in Colorado for an AIA Conference and wasn't able to make the South Carolina trip. Alison, at the same time, was on a business trip to Orlando, but she had the opportunity to fly to South Carolina for the last several days of the Camp and watch her son in the volleyball matches. She and Johnny have shared the love of the game for the past seven or eight years now. Alison continues in coaching girls teams at Legacy Volleyball Club; she knows the game well, is accurately discerning of Johnny's strengths and aspirations, is keenly observant of the play of others and thus she can discuss with excellent insight the points that Johnny voices. Volleyball

Chapter 18

is not the only connection point for open communication that Alison and Johnny share, but it's become a cemented bond of enjoyment for both of them. In a relaxed home setting, it's great to bounce off thoughts and ideas on rehashing and replays of games when respect is mutual. It's a safe environment for both. Mike, too, of course, is quite knowledgeable in the volleyball realm as a coach; the three of them have fun with it all.

Chapter 19

CHANGES

"Therefore if anyone is in Christ, he is a new creature. Old things have passed away; all things have become new."

2 Corinthians 5:17

In the summer of 2019, Hume Lake became the site of the spiritual re-ignition of Johnny's life. Hume Lake is a Christian Camp and Conference Center located in the Sierra Mountain Range in California. It's a place that Johnny knew well. He had been there in previous years as a camper and now he was attending again, for a week, as an incoming High School Senior. He thoroughly enjoyed it there and had been excited about going. He had no idea of what was to come - of the encounter that would bring life altering changes.

    Johnny had been raised all of his life going to Sunday School and Church with his family. His parents, siblings, grandparents, many cousins, aunts and uncles were Christians - people seeking to, with passion and commitment, follow Jesus in their ways of living. Johnny had been an active part of the youth group at the church where he and his family worshiped until his Sophomore year in High School when volleyball practices conflicted with youth group meetings. There was no way to be engaged in both. Gradually, Sunday became a day to catch up on both sleep and homework. Priorities shifted to more consuming volleyball and school friends.

    During his pre-senior year week's camp, something was triggered in his mind and heart that resulted in his changing his habits. Upon his return home, he once again began to attend meetings of the youth group, and eventually assumed a leadership role. Johnny's dedication to Biblical principles of living integrated all facets of his life, and changed his trajectory. I asked him one day if he could tell me what had taken place in his week at Hume Lake that summer of 2019 that made it different from other weeks there in past years. He said something like this. "Even if I had wanted to continue going to Wednesday night youth group, I couldn't have done so because of volleyball practices on the same evenings. So I kind of found myself moving away from church friends and youth involvement. I had always loved Hume Lake and when I got there again this year, I realized how good it felt to be back with friends that I had been close to for years, as well as some of the youth group leaders. Our camp leader challenged us to memorize the verses of John 15:18-27. I put it on my phone so I'd have it with me. In the passage, it talked about "the world hating God." I had felt as though I had been more a part of the world rather than in God's camp. But I knew that I didn't hate God. Hate was such a strong, violent word." He realized that he had a choice to make - and he made the choice to follow Jesus. That decision brought closure to some of his then current friendships, but opened the door to renewal of old and solid friendships of former years. In our family we noticed small changes that gradually became a catalyst to more obviously bold changes that were re-directive to his thinking, his values, his life choices. Johnny's transformational week at Hume Lake continues to drive him into being a solid Christian with a focus on living his life with a passion for growing as a disciple of Christ in all of his ways.

His senior year at West Ranch High from September into March was filled with all of the fun and involvement that is normally part of the aspirations of a senior status. Johnny's world centered around sports, studies, school activities, dating, college applications, hanging out with friends, driving, dances, school services, and for him, church involvement. Life was full and exciting.

Flash forward with me to March 9th of 2020. My husband Bob, Johnny's Papa, was a patient in UCLA's Ronald Reagan Hospital for several days of tests and treatments. I was staying there with him during those days. I had gone to the hospital cafeteria for a bite of lunch one day and I spotted a quiet little corner area that spoke to me of a perfect place to not only take my tray, but to do some writing as well. I had to grab such moments when I could. Within my eye's view, there was a lovely patio with brick inlays, bordered by a well-manicured green lawn which hosted numerous tables with bench seating. I was drawn to the watching of students, to the brisk walking of hospital staff personnel, to visitors sauntering alone along the path, as well as groups of people walking and conversing. Simultaneously, my thoughts began to be reflective of Johnny's senior year at West Ranch and of how quickly the months had gone by and how relatively few weeks remained before he would be a graduate.

Tears welled up in my eyes - tears mingled in emotions of happiness for him, in gratitude that he was standing on the foundation of having lived his life as dynamically, as courageously, as now God-centered as possible. Yet some of those tears had to do with the "letting go" of the little boy that had often been my buddy, my re-entrance into the world of childhood, of playful adventures, of the delights and fascinations of seeing who Johnny was, and of who he was becoming. Those days of impetuous living, of discovery, of laughter and enchantment had led to the privilege of being there during the gradually transformational times of little boy to young boy to young teen, and now he had become a young man who would take paths of his own, unaccompanied by me, or his family.

Chapter 19

And so it is with our beloved children and grandchildren. It is the way of the generations. It is as it should be. It is good; it is right. And though, knowing all of this, my heart still yearned to be a walking companion to see him continue to run forward to embracing all that lay ahead for him. But how shallow love would be if it attempted to hold on, to hold back in any way, that natural desire of our young ones to engage in the sheer joy of the freedom to fly and soar to the heights of all that is possible in a world that is befittingly theirs to capture, one in which they'll be able to serve and make their own contributions, as God grants them vision, strength, love and wisdom. This is indeed my heart's desire for Johnny. He deserves it! He's ready for it!

Chapter 20

A GLOBAL INVASION

"But the Lord stood with me and strengthened me."
2 Timothy 4:17

Days later, a monumental occurrence invaded and altered the course of our lives; not only the lives of our family, but every person and family in our community, city, state, nation and of the entire world. This event was a global disaster, an invasion that was generated by a silent enemy, a vicious, cruel, crippler and destroyer of freedom, and in too many cases, of life itself. Covid-19, a new virus strain, which came to be called The Corona Virus, relentlessly and insidiously, marched across nations, continents, and oceans spreading itself like an invisible caustic pollen in a windstorm that never ceased, only gained in intensity.

Fear gripped our nation as the shocking number of cases of illnesses, hospitalizations, and tragic deaths began to skyrocket and affect every facet of life as it previously had been. Suddenly without warning, schools were closed and education at all grade levels was halted. After several weeks, school classes began to be conducted in an online mode of instruction. Those without computers in their homes were incapable of participating and suffered both educationally and emotionally. Nation after nation began to close their borders in an effort to stay the tide of this virulent virus. Businesses at all levels closed their doors, except for those considered to be essential for maintaining and supplying the basic necessities of life. Most banks, groceries, pharmacies and drug stores continued to function with minimal staffing. Hospitals, law enforcement

Chapter 20

and fire fighting personnel continued on the job, often to the detriment of their own families. Heroes rose out of the ashes of altered ways of performing their duties; brave, courageous, self-sacrificing men and women who forged ahead for the sake of others. Many companies placed their employees on a status of working from home; other employees were placed on furlough, or simply lost their jobs. Unemployment numbers began to soar. Drive-through restaurants flourished and curb-side pickup became a household word. Churches had to close their doors and operate via online streaming. Weddings and funerals had few venues available to them and were limited to barely more than family members in attendance. Neither hospital nor nursing home facilities could admit visitors. Doctors began to evaluate the health and condition of their patients virtually , either a phone chat or a Zoom appointment. The entire world became familiar with the term, "social distancing", the practice of staying six feet apart from others, and the requests and pleas by government and health officials to wear facial masks at all times around others and to wash and sanitize your hands frequently throughout the day. Airline travel ceased, as did Cruise Ship travel. People were generally at home, discovering ways of creatively passing the twenty-four hours of each day. Walkers in neighborhoods increased dramatically. The Center For Disease Control officials teamed with our national President and Vice-President to hold daily briefings via television in an attempt to keep people informed and updated regarding the status of the Pandemic. The challenges were enormous for people all over the world. As the months of Spring went by, and then Summer, then into Fall and Winter, in spite of small victories in seeing some declining numbers in daily cases reported of Covid, signs of other maladies began to become problematic. There remained much yet to conquer!

When Johnny had come home from West Ranch High mid-day on March 13th of 2020, neither he nor we could have imagined that the final quarter of his senior year had really come to a conclusion on a campus site. As the days and weeks went by, classes were reinstated on a non-site status at home, with just you and your computer. Gone were the normal days of the Jr./Sr. Prom, the end of the school year senior trip to Disneyland, the Awards ceremonies, the Sports Banquets, the signing of the yearbooks and all of the other usual celebrations of the senior class of students. Even simple get-togethers with friends weren't possible because of the restrictions of Covid living. Johnny had his first serious girlfriend during his senior year. They did spend time together, either at our house or hers, or sometimes hiking in the nearby hills. I believe that helped them both navigate the weeks and months of "quarantine" that we were all experiencing.

The normal graduation exercises were postponed as the West Ranch leadership staff attempted to put in place that which was acceptable according to state guidelines. In the end, in June of the year, West Ranch held a "drive-by" graduation ceremony for seniors at a local park, with robed students departing cars driven by their families, who halted driving for the several minutes that it took for their graduate to leave the car and ascend the wooden ramp to the newly built platform to accept their diploma from the school administrator. Later in the summer, a televised awards ceremony was available to be viewed via live streaming. Names of recipients of special awards were announced. Johnny was the recipient of the National Marine Corps Award honoring Meritorious Valor. Only one graduate received this annual award.

West Ranch High School had distributed good-looking CONGRATULATORY lawn posters to each family who had requested one. Each poster had the name and picture of the

Chapter 20

graduate. Other high schools across the Santa Clarita Valley were doing the same thing. It was a small token of commemoration, a visible sign out on the lawn for all to see. Under the prevailing Covid restrictions, it was perhaps the best that high schools could offer. Johnny was well aware of how extraordinarily proud we were of him and of his unique and brave accomplishments, not because of a poster, but because we told him so often.

His older sister, Emily, had graduated from Pepperdine University in Malibu, CA in May of 2020, Pepperdine had chosen to postpone any graduation exercises. We weren't encouraged to gather as a greater family because of Covid restrictions, so our family organized a Celebration Drive-by of family members in their cars, some decorated for the occasion with balloons, with music blaring and posters and gifts for her. She was surprised and pleased. She had excelled as an honor student, graduating in only three years, while working at the same time. We were so proud of her and of her accomplishments. Two family graduates of higher education in the ill-fated Covid year, both having to adjust to a "new norm" - perhaps only temporarily. Only God knows that outcome with accuracy. That which we do know is that Johnny's creativity and positive attitude were instrumental in the way in which he both accepted and navigated the many months of the quarantining at home which were necessitated by Covid-19 living. He's a very social guy, but somehow he managed to stay optimistic in a world where socializing had to be limited to your small family "bubble", and to phone communication with friends. One of his most creative projects was in converting our dining room into AN ESCAPE ROOM in order to celebrate his brother, Christopher's 25th birthday. Escape Rooms were prevalent out in the marketplace, drawing the teen-age and young adult crowd in vast numbers. Johnny did an absolutely phenomenal job in designing a set-up that turned out to be extremely difficult for an escape in the time allotment. Out in the communities, it would have competed well. His Papa Bob was so impressed with Johnny's resourcefulness that he offered to back him in any future aspirational business ventures. Bob was a wise discerner of unusual talent when he saw it. He also was an economics professor. And he was a proud and loving grandpa.

    Volleyball, the passion of Johnny's life, ceased, as did all organized sports. The world became a sobering place; anxiety and depression would be on the increase in some lives. It was a "time that would try the souls of men and women".

Chapter 21

Sorrow Strikes

"He will not be shaken by bad tidings; his heart is steadfast, trusting in the Lord".

Psalm 112:7

Throughout the winter and spring months of 2020, Johnny's grandfather, his Papa Bob, battled illness upon illness which led to his having to be hospitalized for the last seven weeks of his life. Due to Covid restrictions, none of us in the family were able to be with him, except via Zoom. On July 2nd of 2020, God lovingly relieved his suffering and took him home to His Heaven. We were thankful that he suffered no more, but my own personal loss of him was devastating and painful beyond my comprehension. We had been married for sixty-five years. Our children and our grandchildren were experiencing hearts that ached and hurt. Bob had been an ardent, on site, fan of Johnny's numerous athletic and academic award involvements throughout the years, traveling with me to Ohio, Arizona, Texas and Southern California sites to watch him play volleyball. Johnny and his Papa Bob's lives were intertwined. Bob had recognized in Johnny, not only an outstanding athletic talent, but an extraordinarily intelligent and resourceful mind. He often spoke of Johnny's kind heart, a heart that had faithfully translated into action in helping us in bringing suitcases or heavy groceries into our home on his own initiative. He helped us in some way almost daily. Johnny had always shown a deep love, honor and admiration for his Papa Bob.

There was an enormous hole in our home without Bob's

towering strength of Godliness, his wisdom, his humor, his music, his warmth of encouragement and love. His lasting gifts to all of us in the entire family were deeply embedded in our hearts. We had all watched him, as faithfully and with integrity through the years, he had lived a life of vigor, adventure, family-centeredness and Godly commitment and influence, demonstrating over and over again a joy in generosity and sacrificial love. In the last two years of his life, we had watched him as he navigated debilitating and humbling health issues with a spirit of optimism, never complaining, only evidencing a trust in God's Grace and Goodness. His heart's desire was that his loved ones would know of his strong belief "that without a test, you have no real testimony". He lived that testimony out to his last breath, so well, so very, very well. Johnny, already in young adulthood, has been tested and proven to be living out a testimony to God's faithfulness. Grandfather and grandson, united in a heart's pursuit!

  In the days and weeks following his Papa's death, Johnny's hugs to me were affectionately warm, lingering and tight. His ever present kindness shone through his eyes and transferred into unspoken actions of helpfulness that said far more than words could have of the recognition of my sorrow, and of his own hurting heart. Johnny was dealing with his first Augur family loss of one that he loved dearly. It was a tender summer for him.

  One day at summer's end, our entire California family came to our home. We held a little ceremony of placing the cloth Levi, newsboy style hat, that Bob had worn regularly during the last year of his life, on the cross in our backyard. When I was a young girl, there was a popular expression: "I'd hang my hat on it". It meant that it was an absolutely sure thing. You could count on it. We knew with all certainty in every heart gathered

Chapter 21

there that day, that our beloved Bob was now in Heaven, experiencing all of the glories of which God had written and promised. The hat was our way of expressing a sealing recognition and honor of the depth of our love and cherishment of him and of our own certainty of the truth of Heaven. We placed his hat on top of the wooden cross that Johnny had fashioned, the one in recent years that bore the collars of Deja and Shadow, the dear Labrador pets that had been part of the growing up years of the kids. Johnny nailed the hat to the cross so that the strong winds so prevalent in our area wouldn't blow the hat away. Bob had dearly loved both Deja and Shadow, and they him. The cross seemed a perfect place for his final favorite, well-worn hat to rest. The hat seemed to have had a voice; through it, God had spoken into our grief and into our trusting faith.

Chapter 22

OFF TO THE FUTURE

"For I know the plans I have for you; plans to take care of you; plans to give you the future you hope for."
Jeremiah 29:11 (The Message)

The University of Hawaii had opened its doors to Johnny for admission and possibly an opportunity to play volleyball. But that was "iffy" and brought with it the uncertainty of when Covid restrictions would be lifted for team sports. Fall semester classes were scheduled to be conducted on an online status only, and perhaps Spring classes as well. Johnny made the decision to stay in Santa Clarita and enroll in a local Junior College rather than incurring thousands of dollars in debts for housing and out-of-state tuition to enroll in online courses and be engaged in quarantined living. We were in agreement that it was a smart decision on his part.

As a college freshman attending a local Junior College, Johnny lived at home, taking all classes online. It wasn't at all a collegiate dream, but it was happening in a similar fashion all across the world. No on-campus classes, no organized sports, no social gatherings. Exercising was reduced to workouts at home, hikes, bicycling and miles of walking. These were the physical fitness tools of the Pandemic. For athletes who were trying to stay in shape in the midst of gradually increasing sedentary lifestyles, it was necessary to be diligent in determination to stay disciplined to the basic principles of athleticism.

Chapter 22

In July of the year, an opportunity of a part time job at a Canine Camp in the area opened up for Johnny. The hours would be compatible with his college classes and he readily accepted the job. It proved to be a great fit for him; he loved working with the forty or so dogs that were boarded there on the grounds. In a way they became his new friends; he would have humorous stories to tell of the playfulness and antics of the interactions of the dogs. His care and protection of them included killing any rattlesnakes that might present a danger to them. Rattlesnakes are prevalent in the early spring/summer climate of Southern California. The workers at the Canine Camp were trained in how to properly use the equipment to both catch and kill the snakes. In the late Spring of 2021, Johnny had encountered several rattlesnakes that he had killed, bringing home the rattles as his trophies This job requirement was unsettling to me. I dealt with it in the only way I knew how to do so - with passionate prayer for God's protection of Johnny, and most particularly with rattlesnake encounters. One day, he came home with a video on his phone of his confrontation with a very large rattlesnake that was hiding underneath the house of the owner of the Camp. It posed a threat to the dogs, so Johnny, without proper clothing protection, bravely crawled in the darkness, under the house for a distance of about twenty feet with a flashlight in one hand and a pair of snake tongs in the other hand. Natalie, his cousin and co-worker, was videoing from a safe position near the house as this was happening; she saw the size of the snake from her protected spot at about the time that Johnny spotted it and heard the sound of the rattle. The snake was large. Quickly and with brave precision, he grabbed the snake behind the head with the tongs and then crawled backwards in the dark with the snake in tow until he was out from under the house and could stand up. Natalie was waiting with a shovel to cut off the head of the snake. Johnny had to admit that this conquest had left him a bit shaken. He was not a professional snake handler. He was a dog camp worker, simply doing what needed to be done by someone who had the courage to do so. It's the type of courage forged in the grit and grind of facing the giants in your life, whether they be dangerous situations or temptations to succumb to fears of the "what ifs" that could render you inept. It's the kind of courage that results in victorious living and makes heroes of young and old alike. Later in the day, he and Natalie skinned the snake. Johnny brought the meat home to cook, as well as the nine rattles. The skin is in his room - a handsome trophy if it doesn't give you nightmares, like it did this Grandma. Needless to say, my prayers for Johnny's safety on the job increased to a new level of intensity.

  One of the prized gifts of his job at the dog camp came to our home in the form of a beautiful little eight year old dog, Kiba, who bounced into our lives with all of the love, fun and loyalty possible. Kiba became a life-saving therapy dog for me during the months and years after the loss of my husband. He was a miracle gift from Johnny's boss to give to me in my time of upheaval and great sorrow. I saw her generosity as an act of love that demonstrated her high regard and appreciation for Johnny as a dedicated, faithful, valued employee. Kiba has captured the hearts of our entire family.

  The job at the Canine Camp paid well. Due to a minimal social life and quarantined living, Johnny was able to save funds to purchase a used truck. With that behind him, he then had thoughts of saving some of his earnings for a college fund for his Junior and Senior years when he possibly would be transferring to San Diego State University. It was a good plan, but it became apparent that God had an even better plan, as He often does in

Chapter 22

our lives. Scripture tells us that "A man's heart plans his way, but the Lord directs his steps." (Proverbs 16:9)

For the past year or so, Mike had been serving as a chaplain and assistant men's volleyball coach for Masters University, in Newhall, CA, not far from our home. Masters is an excellent university, based on Biblical, Christian life principles. The school established a men's volleyball team several years ago. Johnny and the new, incoming Head Coach connected at a game one day. The coach invited him to try out at several of the team's practice sessions. Johnny revved up his game as hard as he could in the short time available to him. Even though he hadn't been able to really play for an entire year, the Masters coach liked what he saw on the court. He expressed his desire to see him come aboard for the upcoming season's play, contingent of course upon his enrollment as a student at Masters. Almost before you could turn around, Johnny had completed and submitted the application for admittance. In addition, he had applied for scholarship aid. Soon, he received a confirmation of both his admittance to Masters and of a generous scholarship assistance. God had opened a door and Johnny had walked right through it in seizing the opportunity with a grateful heart. He plunged in to carve out early morning hours, before work, to do weight training sessions as well as routine gym workout times with some of the volleyball teammates, thus already forming friendships with players, and demonstrating his energy and passion as an incoming team member.

The graciousness of God in being The Potter who is tenderly forming Johnny into a young man whose heart yearns to bring honor to his God, is a crowning gift that speaks into His Kingdom purpose for Johnny's life. Johnny knows whose Hand has been upon him all of these years to bring him to the point of where he stands today. He's tremendously grateful for the blessing of being one who has benefitted from the Cystic Fibrosis breakthroughs in recent years of targeted medications geared towards a better quality of life. His heart of kindness towards others has come, I believe in large part, from knowing what it feels like to live with a lifelong progressive genetic disease. This kinship has generated his desire to spur others onward in their quests for life's fulfillment.

Chapter 23
CATCH THE VISION

"Let us run with strength and zeal the race that is set before us."
Hebrews 12:1

We've come to June of the year of 2021. Final exams brought a conclusion to Johnny's freshman year of college. Three days after finals, he was on a plane bound for Honolulu to vacation with several friends who live there whom he met while playing volleyball in South Carolina. He made all of the travel arrangements and now is enjoying, with full vigor, a ten day celebration. He's gone back to the place where he was born nineteen years ago, back to his roots. When he left with his family to move to Southern California, he was not quite two and a half. At that point in time, the uncertainty of the quality of his life as a little boy who needed to deal with the rigors of living and battling Cystic Fibrosis loomed large.

The years have been kind in giving Johnny life, an unbelievable life in many ways. Months have passed since the beginning days of Covid and all of the parameters of living that were associated with the Pandemic Johnny is now a sophomore student at Masters University. He's in his second semester and thoroughly immersed in campus life there. He has found the classes to be provocative. His mind is being stretched as he grapples with new concepts and subject matter. He can articulate well the reason why he believes something, or he can disagree well, with respect, with someone who has a different viewpoint. He is an attentive listener as well as a notable communicator. His mind is open, curious, questioning, validating his innate leadership skills.

Johnny's dream of playing collegiate volleyball has come true! He's first string setter on the men's varsity team and he's playing phenomenal ball. He's a team leader of the finest caliber, while giving all glory to God, never to himself. He continues to inspire me daily. Spiritually, his faith has never been more fierce; he's living his life as an ongoing testimony to the transformations that have taken place in the last few years. Many friends, family members and prayer groups have held him in their hearts for prayer throughout the years; prayers for strengthening of his health with healing. We couldn't have imagined how powerful these prayers would be in the results that have occurred. God has listened - and responded in the most phenomenal ways possible. Our thanksgiving is to Him!

When I commenced to write this story about Johnny, he was only ten years old. I began the work because I thought his story, even at such a young age, needed to be told, a story that could inspire others, and he was too young to do so himself. On September seventh of 2022, we celebrated his twenty-first birthday. I have given you a mere glimpse, from this grandmother's perspective, of his life into his twenty-first year, launching into his twenty-second. The rest of his life will be his story to tell. He will tell it by actions and impact, leaving others to describe and emulate his remarkable influence upon their own lives.

Johnny's unique impact upon people, his ability for reaching and inspiring others, is a channeling force to inspire those youth and their families who live under the potentially discouraging mantle of Cystic Fibrosis dominance. The story of his life from infancy to adulthood can speak profoundly into other lives, igniting rays of hope, and beacons of motivational

Chapter 23

help in rising above the circumstances of your life to defeat man's predictions and claim victories. I believe him to be a pioneer in the world of Cystic Fibrosis, pushing himself beyond limits to physical success, living passionately, energetically with drive and focus. But this has not happened without hard work on his part in sticking to the rigors of the dedicated treatments that have been his commitment.

It has been said that behind every successful husband is an ardent and successful wife. It has also been said that behind every corporate leader is a phenomenal secretary. In Johnny's case, I believe that there are three extraordinaries: his God, his parents and his own courage. His parents first of all gave him the facts of what was necessary to do medically as well as the constant help, support and encouragement to follow through: then they gave him the freedom to live his life fully, to soar to the heights of all that Johnny could envision. God gave him not only the vision of a phenomenal life, but His Presence, His Holy Spirit and His anointing strength to accomplish it. Johnny had the drive, the passion and the courage to break the boundaries of CF living - and to be engaged in living way beyond the norm. I believe that his life will be noteworthy in inspiring many who struggle just to keep going each day. Valiant efforts have the lively promise of rewards, hope begets hope, success breeds success. Johnny's extraordinary story of courage, of living life so well, for one so young, can be a life-changing catalyst to others in need.

Thus far, Johnny has defied every dire prediction of books, journals and stories of many who have dealt with Cystic Fibrosis. His spunk and spirit as a youngster caused him to live life as an overcomer. His joy in just being alive has given him a drive to press on, to live life fully in the moment. He refuses to accept cautious limitations imposed by others who approach life in a more timid manner. If there has been a way to do something, he has worked hard to find it or develop it. His intelligence and resourcefulness are intertwined to the point of success. Yet he accepts with humility the awards and recognitions that he has received. Boasting is never his to do. He lets his actions and the way he lives his life speak for themselves. I love remembering Johnny's bold laugh, his witty comebacks, his loyalty to his close friends and his boisterous exuberance. He has battled hard with diligence, fortitude, and determination to not let Cystic Fibrosis dominate in any way who he is or what he accomplishes. He is MY HERO in every sense of the word!

    I realize that some of Johnny's personality and strong characteristics are genetic in nature. They are God-given. But other strengths of his have been forged by his own drive and determination to live passionately, with courage, with humor, with joy, zest and an innate resourcefulness to not only be the best that he can possibly be, by God's grace, but to share and look out with kindness and love and help for his fellow man. Just this past week, on August 2nd of 2022, we learned of the passing of Vince Scully, the infamous voice and soul of the Los Angeles Dodgers, a man loved and respected by generations of people. His desire, according to family reports, was to be known as a man of integrity, grace and honesty. He accomplished that! By God's good grace, Johnny had been invited to go to Dodger Stadium last night, as the guest of a friend, to see the honoring of this beloved man of baseball, a role model to thousands of announcers and fans. Honorable role models can serve a great purpose in our lives.

    I have learned much from my grandson Johnny about the matters of life and heart that are truly important. His

Chapter 23

extraordinary ways will forever be a part of the deepest part of me. I can't wait to see what lies ahead for him in the days to come. His spirit is indomitable, his vision is unlimited, his drive and talents are truly a force of nature. Johnny's anchored message is that his story has not occurred by his own strength, but by the will of God that has given him the strength to overcome, thus far, whatever life has thrown at him. "All of the glory is for HIS name's sake"!

My story of Johnny concludes with these words to him: "Go for it Johnny! Keep pushing the boundaries to catch all of your dreams. You're the warrior setter with the ball. Keep breaking those records, honey, on and off the court. You're also the messenger/discipler of the God of all creation. Keep drawing people to HIS throne! This Grandma loves you so much". "See ya"!

Chapter 24

THE JOURNEY FORWARD

"Reaching forward to those things which lie ahead, I press toward the goal of the upward call of God in Christ Jesus".
Philippians 3:13-14

When Cystic Fibrosis became more than just a medical term to be defined, and we came face-to-face with our beloved grandson's battle to conquer this devastating disease, we moved with passion and determination to do what we could to help in the cause of raising dollars for research that would bring breakthroughs in finding a cure one day. We connected with the Cystic Fibrosis Foundation in our local area and became volunteers in helping with the various fundraising events each year which included golf tournaments, silent and live auctions, wine tasting events, along with other offerings.. The Cystic Fibrosis Foundation is the leading organization committed to finding new therapies for CF, and to improving the lives of those with the disease. Its mission is to cure Cystic Fibrosis and to provide all people with CF the opportunity to lead long, fulfilling lives by funding research and drug development, partnering with the CF community, and advancing high-quality, specialized care. "Adding tomorrows to every day" is not just a slogan on paper designed and illuminated by the Cystic Fibrosis Foundation; it is a present reality that has been forged with consistency and dedication, and continues to be a successful driving force to transformational living to those who deal specifically with Cystic Fibrosis.

For about fifteen years, Bob and I were driven towards involvement in helping to raise dollars for research and to bring awareness of the disease of Cystic Fibrosis to the forefront of the minds and hearts of people locally, and even nationally. Our time, our resources, our energy were poured out in the cause to see breakthroughs and cures developed that would bring significant improvement in quality of life to thousands of people who were under the bondage to the ramifications of living their lives with Cystic Fibrosis. But our passion, first and foremost, continued to be our overriding desire and commitment to linking with all our hearts to do whatever it took to walk with our family each day in total support and encouragement and helping hands that said, "we are here for you all the way". I believe it's the greatest gift that we all can give to one another – the gift of ourselves, of demonstrating love, the gift of dedicated and fervent prayer, the gift of standing strong with someone as they walk through the most difficult trials of life. To be there even when you're exhausted and feel you have no energy left except to remember that your loved one carries an even greater burden and desperately needs your help, your strength, your understanding, your feet and hands and arms of love. These are the gifts that can make a difference in pressing on, in running the race, in finishing strong and standing with someone so that they don't feel alone in the fight – to help bring strength for each day and a shining hope for tomorrow.

There is a slogan that is used frequently in the literature put out by the Cystic Fibrosis Foundation. The slogan is "Help Add Tomorrows Every Day"! When the CF Foundation began in 1955, few children with CF lived to attend elementary school. Today, the median age of survival for a person with CF extends into the mid forties and beyond. Research is making a real difference, however precious lives continue to be lost, and the quality of life for those who suffer the ravages of this disease is in need of improvement. The CF Foundation has developed more than ten treatments - an unprecedented number in a short span of time adding decades of life to those with CF. Every contribution and donation made by generous hearts counts. Every breath is precious. Johnny himself is participating in a fifteen month long clinical trial which is testing the advocacy of a new, targeted medication for CF improvement. This is the second clinical trial in which he has been involved.

The Cystic Fibrosis Foundation is an organization of energy and integrity. Almost 90% of all monies raised go directly to research at major universities across the United States as well as to funding a nationwide network of more than 115 specialty care centers dedicated to treating people with CF. It is said that "Most of the things worth doing in the world had been declared impossible before they were done." One mother didn't believe in the impossibility factor. Her name was Mary G. Weiss and she became a volunteer for the Cystic Fibrosis Foundation in 1965 after learning that her three little boys had Cystic Fibrosis. Her duty was to call every civic club, social and service organization, seeking financial support for Cystic Fibrosis research. Mary's four-year-old son, Richard, listened closely to his mother as she made each call. After several calls, Richard came into the room and told his mom, "I know what you are working for." Mary was dumbstruck because Richard did not know what she was doing, nor did he know that he had Cystic Fibrosis. With some trepidation, Mary posed the question back to Richard, "What am I working for, Richard?" "You are working for "65 Roses," he answered sweetly. Mary was speechless. She went over to him and tenderly pressed his tiny body to hers. He could not see the tears running down Mary's cheeks as she stammered. "Yes, Richard, I'm working for 65 Roses." "65 Roses" is what little children suffering from cystic fibrosis often call their disease. The words are much easier for children to pronounce.

Chapter 24

Since 1955, the term "65 Roses" has been used by children of all ages to describe their disease. But, making it easier to say does not make CF any easier to live with. The "65 Roses" story has captured the hearts and emotions of all who have heard it. The rose, appropriately the ancient symbol of love, has become a symbol of the Cystic Fibrosis Foundation. Johnny has a single rose tattoo on his upper arm signifying his dedication to the cure-targeted work of the Cystic Fibrosis Foundation

To those of you who have read this book, and who are living with CF, it is my passionate hope and prayer that Johnny's story will provide help on your journey. May your own breaths that are so vital, so precious, be deepened, strengthened and enhanced as one young man's story is unveiled. May you find in the book's pages a tangible inspiration to take hold of and step into with a new vision, courage, dedication and hope. And ultimately, because someone needs it, may the story of your life inspire and help others. Whether it's CF or something else in your life that is continually challenging you, may you, like Johnny and his family, find strength and courage through the transforming power of a life centered in and upon God the Father, Son and Holy Spirit. And may that trust and faith in action be a catalyst to your becoming an "overcomer", and a contributor to helping others along this journey that we call life.

EPILOGUE

A number of recent events have occurred which are relevant to Johnny's current life. I feel compelled to tell you of them because I believe that as readers, you and I and Johnny have formed a friendship of sorts through your interest and perseverance in reading our book. It is my joy to share these special happenings with you.

One of them has to do with his achievements as a starting setter on the Master's University Men's Volleyball team. As a freshman setter this past year, Johnny broke the existing records of Master's University for number of assists by a setter in any single match as well as single-season program records for assists.

His season's overall accomplishments led to an article, written by his volleyball coach, who submitted it to the CalHope organization. They in turn named Johnny as a CalHope Courage award winner for April of 2022. CalHOPE recognizes and honors student athletes at California colleges and universities each month for overcoming the stress, anxiety, and mental trauma associated with personal hardships, injury, or life circumstances who can inspire others and make a difference in lives. The coach's words follow.

"CalHope Courage award winner for April, 2022, Johnny Buchanan, a freshman on the Master's University men's volleyball team, has not let Cystic Fibrosis (CF), nor being immunocompromised in the age of Covid, prevent him from developing his mind and body. His condition has always made sports difficult, even before Covid, because CF has an adverse effect on lungs, cardiovascular health, growth, and life expectancy. However the pandemic presented additional challenges for Johnny Buchanan, who has lived his whole life understanding that he is always at risk. When Covid hit in the middle of his senior year at West Ranch High School in Valencia, California, it disrupted his college and volleyball plans. He decided to attend a local community college, where he did not play volleyball, before transferring this year to The Master's University. Through his strong Christian faith, Johnny has stayed resilient mentally through the numerous challenges caused by his CF, including isolation from peers when needing to undergo multiple breathing treatments a day. He prays, reads his Bible, and regularly attends church services to bring him peace and comfort in the trials he faces. On the court, he was the starting setter on the nation's 12th ranked National Association of Intercollegiate Athletics (NAIA) men's volleyball team, finishing fourth in the Golden State Athletic Conference (GSAC) in assists/set, while setting single-match and single-season program records for assists. He helped lead the Mustangs to a 13-11 record and a berth in the GSAC championship game, where their magical run ended with a loss to Ottawa University in Arizona. In the classroom, the Kinesiology and Physical Education major has recorded straight A's, managing to find a balance of living his life while taking precautions to stay safe.

"While the rest of the world has seen the dangers of COVID the past couple of years, this is really all I've ever known," said Buchanan, who is a native of Honolulu. "That first year of college, I realized how much I missed competing and the grind of training. Coming to The Master's University has allowed me to continue my desire to develop my body, mind and spirit for the glory of Christ".

Another article, written by the Master's University Assistant Athletic Director, reads in part. "For all that Johnny has overcome and the perseverance displayed in the face of trials, Buchanan was one of three collegiate student athletes to receive the CalHOPE Award for courage for the month of April. His coach has written that he continues to persevere and set an example to his teammates, friends and everyone he encounters. "It's an honor to win an award for courage", Buchanan said. "Courage is a command from the Lord in Joshua 1:9, so it's encouraging to see that others recognize my living out of the commands of the Lord. Faith has been the foundation of how I overcome my trials", Buchanan said. "Ever since the Lord has cleared my eyes of the sinful desires of my flesh, I have counted all trials as joy and used them in a way to glorify and worship the Lord. I hope that what anyone takes away from my story is that it was not by my own strength, but by the will of God that I have the strength to overcome whatever life seems to throw at me". Buchanan said, "All the glory is for HIS name's sake".

We, in our family, as well as others who have known, loved and prayed for him, are jubilant as well as so proud of this latest honor. He has labored diligently in the face of difficult circumstances like the courageous warrior that he is. Once again, he has, with humility, accepted this recognition with a grateful heart as a blessing from God, as well as an opportunity to bring glory and honor to his Lord and Savior.

The second occurrence that I want to tell you about is Johnny's desire to "pay forward" his talent of volleyball skills by helping others to learn, play and organize competitive games in the communities of South India. He and his parents left in mid-May of 2022 on a two week mission trip dedicated to that effort, as well as to spreading the gospel of the good news of

Epilogue

Jesus Christ. Johnny at age almost 21, is demonstrating a life that reflects not only his extraordinary courage, but also his desire to be a light that will draw others to the foot of the Cross. Selah!

One last story that I desire to recount took place on August 31st of 2022. In a temperature setting of around 108 degrees, a massive brush fire exploded that would in a short time become a raging wildfire that would threaten over 5,000 acres of parched hillside land. It was given the name of the Route fire. The Castaic Canine Camp, where Johnny worked part time, was in the general area of the fire. Hundreds of firefighters were on the job to save homes and property as well as tankers dropping as much water as possible. At the conclusion of a day of University classes, Johnny saw the burgeoning smoke and learned of the fire's location. He jumped into his truck and headed towards the dog camp. All major access roads were closed due to the fire. Johnny drove on obscure canyon roads which connected to other roads and eventually he arrived at the rather remote camp, having traveled through thick smoke when sight was barely visible. He helped the owner and several on-site workers to evacuate the dogs to a safe location at which point owners could pick them up. He then loaded five of the owner's dogs, in their crates, into his truck and with a police escort a portion of the way, drove them to safety: safety resided at our house. Sixty hours later, the dogs were still with us, because the fire's embers had not been vanquished. Johnny's compromised lungs had taken a secondary place in his heart and thinking; he had sacrificed his own health in order to rescue the dogs. Never backing down, the courage to break boundaries had once again prevailed.

Acknowledgements

Manuscripts are seldom put into print, into a book form that reaches the reader, without tremendous help, support and encouragement from others. My great cloud of witnesses, my support team, has been strong and faithful over these last ten years. During slack times, when life crowded in to embrace mountain peak experiences or downward spirals of deep, dark valley encounters, their encouragement never waned. To all of you, and you know who you are, I gladly and humbly give my heart full of thanks for your consistency of interest, your time spent on your knees in prayer and your endless demonstrations of encouragement. Most particularly, there are three whose help and partnership have made this book a reality.

To our son, Bob. Bob stepped in to take the rough, raw pages of my manuscript, then scrutinized, edited, reformatted, inserted pictures, and artistically and thoughtfully designed the entirety of the book, as well as the cover. Without Bob's dedicated partnership with me in the sharing of his remarkable talent, and the generosity of endless hours of his time, which he lovingly and freely offered, there would be no book today. There would be only memories in my head. Bob has made my dream come true - the story of Johnny's life to date. This is the fourth published book that he has done for our family. I am thankful beyond all words for his innate gifts of artistry, help and love. I love you, Bob, with all of my heart. Your Dad is smiling in full measure, I know, and applauding his talented son.

To our daughter, Alison, Johnny's mother, who read and re-read the manuscript for accuracy and integrity of my 88-year old memory. She also did the tedious work of locating the pictures that are included in the text . This was not a quick hunt but rather a devoted search which she tucked into her already full days of having her own regular two jobs as well as an insanely busy life. I am overwhelmingly grateful for your taking upon yourself my work as though it were your own, Alison. Your positivity, optimism, fully engaged and incredibly loving relationship with your son have been huge factors in helping to shape his life into becoming the phenomenal young man that he is today. I love you dearly, our beautiful, sunshine daughter and thank you with every fiber of my being for your total trust in me to pen the story of your beloved son. Another Big Smile from your Dad along with a "that's my girl" applause.

To our son-in-law, Mike - Johnny's dad whose love for and belief in his son as an extremely talented athlete and bright young man consistently undergirded Johnny in his many endeavors, not the least of which was investing heavily in modeling Christian character to his son and backing him in encouraging Johnny to live his life fully, without fear, to the honor and glory of God.

An Invitation

As Johnny's parents we would love to talk with you about anything that you have read in this book...thoughts, questions, or concerns that were raised or alleviated. We obviously don't know everything about CF, but we do know our own experience and would be honored to walk along side you in your journey.

Please feel free to contact us at:

couragebeyondpassion@gmail.com

- Alison & Mike Buchanan

Notations

PROLOGUE	1) "If You've Got A Dream, Chase It" from the album, "Till You Can't" by Cody Johnson
	2) "If You Can Dream It, You Can Do It" by Tom Fitzgerald, an imagineer of the Walt Disney Corporation, written specifically for the Horizons attraction at Epcot
CHAPTER 1	"The spirit of God has made me, and the breath of the Almighty gives me life". Job 33:4, New Kings James Version, Spirit Filled Life Bible; Thomas Nelson Publisher, Copyright 1991
CHAPTER 2	"Your hands have made me and fashioned me, an intricate unity. You have granted me life and favor, and your care has preserved my spirit". Job 10: 8, 12 IBID
CHAPTER 3	"Whatever your hand finds to do, do it with all your might". Ecclesiastes 9:10 IBID
CHAPTER 4	"Be ready in season and out of season". 2 Timothy 4:2 IBID
CHAPTER 5	"He who is of a merry heart has a continual feast. Life is a banquet when one is joyful". Proverbs 15:15 IBID
CHAPTER 6	1) "And a little child shall lead them". Isaiah 11:6 IBID
	2) "Have mercy on me, O Lord, for I am weak; O Lord, heal me, for my bones are troubled". Psalm 6:2 IBID
CHAPTER 7	"Rejoice young man in your youth and let your heart cheer you in the days of your youth". Ecclesiastes 11:9 IBID
CHAPTER 8	"Let no one not respect your youth, but be an example to the believers in word, in conduct, in love, in spirit, in faith, in purity". 1 Timothy 4:12 IBID
CHAPTER 9	1) "So the child grew and became strong in spirit. Luke 1:80 IBID
	2) "The Lord is my shepherd, I shall not want. He makes me to lie down in green pasture. . . . He restores my soul". Psalm 23:1-2 IBID
CHAPTER 10	"Blessed are the people who know the joyful sound". Psalm 89:15 IBID
CHAPTER 11	"Faith is the substance of things hoped for, the evidence of things not yet seen". Hebrews 11:1 IBID
CHAPTER 12	"And whatever you do, do it heartily, as to the Lord and not to men". Colossians 3:23 IBID

CHAPTER 13	"You shall eat in plenty and be satisfied and praise the name of the Lord your God who has dealt wondrously with you". Joel 2:26 IBID
CHAPTER 14	"The Lord has done great things for us and we are glad". Psalm 126:3 IBID
CHAPTER 15	"Behold, I will do a new thing. Now it shall spring forth". Isaiah 43:18 IBID
CHAPTER 16	"Wait on the Lord. Be of good courage, and He shall strengthen your heart". Psalm 27:14 IBID
CHAPTER 17	"Do you see a man who excels in his work' he will stand before kings". Proverbs 22:29 IBID
CHAPTER 18	"The Lord is with you, you mighty man of valor". Judges 6:12 IBID
CHAPTER 19	"Therefore, if anyone is in Christ, he is a new creature. Old things have passed away; all things have become new". 2 Corinthians 5:17 IBID
CHAPTER 20	"But the Lord stood with me and strengthened me". 2 Timothy 4:17 IBID
CHAPTER 21	"He will not be shaken by bad tidings; his heart is steadfast, trusting in the Lord". Psalm 112:7 IBID
CHAPTER 22	1) "For I know the plans I have for you; plans to take care of you; plans to give you the future you hope for". Jeremiah 29:11 The Message. Biblia.com 2) "A man's heart plans his way, but the Lord directs his steps". Proverbs 16:9 New King James Version, Spirit Filled Life Bible; Thomas Nelson Publisher, Copyright 1991
CHAPTER 23	"Let us run with strength and zeal the race that is set before us". Hebrews 12:1 IBID
CHAPTER 24	"Reaching forward to those things which lie ahead, I press toward the goal of the upward call of God in Christ Jesus." Philippians 3:13-14 IBID

Made in the USA
Columbia, SC
19 February 2023